Effective Teamwork

MICHAEL D. MAGINN

The Business Skills Express Series

IRWIN

Professional Publishing /**MIRROR PRESS**

Burr Ridge, Illinois
New York, New York

© RICHARD D. IRWIN, INC., 1994

This publication is designed to provide accurate and authoritative information in regard to the subject matter covered. It is sold with the understanding that neither the author nor the publisher is engaged in rendering legal, accounting, or other professional service. If legal advice or other expert assistance is required, the services of a competent professional person should be sought.

From a Declaration of Principles jointly adopted by a Committee of the American Bar Association and a Committee of Publishers.

Mirror Press:	David R. Helmstadter
	Carla F. Tishler
Editor-in-Chief:	Jeffrey A. Krames
Project editor:	Stephanie M. Britt
Production manager:	Diane Palmer
Designer:	Jeanne M. Rivera
Art coordinator:	Heather Burbridge
Illustrator:	Boston Graphics, Inc.
Compositor:	Alexander Graphics
Typeface:	12/14 Criterion
Printer:	Malloy Lithographing, Inc.

Library of Congress Cataloging-in-Publication Data

Maginn, Michael D.
   Effective teamwork / Michael D. Maginn.
     p.   cm.—(Business skills express)
    ISBN 1-55623-880-0 (alk. paper)
    1. Work groups.   2. Decision-making.   I. Title.
  HD66.M345   1994
  658.4'036—dc20   93–5

Printed in the United States of America
4 5 6 7 8 9 0   ML   0 9 8 7 6 5

PREFACE

SO LONG, HIERARCHY

It seems like only yesterday. People called *bosses* made decisions and handed them down to other people called *workers,* who did what the bosses said. The bosses decided what to do, how to do it, and how well everyone was doing at doing what the bosses said to do. Not only did workers expect to be told what to do, many workers never openly questioned the boss–worker hierarchy or contributed their opinions. Workers became skilled at whatever tasks they performed, and they were expected to continue doing what they did best until someone told them to do things differently. That was how businesses and organizations were managed since before the start of the Industrial Revolution. Doing things through top-down control and authority worked successfully for a long, long time. Until, in case you haven't noticed, just a few years ago.

Now, the old way of managing is broken. Why? In a nutshell, businesses—and many other types of organizations—have become too complicated, too dependent on expanding information, esoteric expertise, and state-of-the-art technology, too fast-moving and ever-changing. They are too big to understand, let alone manage, by giving orders. Bosses are no longer smart enough to know, control, improve, oversee, and approve everything. Many a company has lost hard-earned market share to new, nontraditional, or emboldened competition, while stubbornly holding to that relic, the pyramid-shaped Organization Chart.

HELLO, TEAM

To deal with these incredibly rapid shifts and intense competitive pressures, many businesses, organizations, and institutions have fundamentally restructured how things get done. Now, *teams* of employees make decisions about what to do and how to do it. Top management has recognized what workers had already sensed—that employees close to the real workings of an enterprise have the expertise, information, and perspective to make a difference, especially when they work cooperatively together and pool their resources. Through teams of all kinds and at all levels, employees solve problems, improve processes, develop products, even manage themselves in some cases, and otherwise make the business work effectively. The world of managing has shifted from Top-Down to Push Down.

WELCOME TO EFFECTIVE TEAMWORK

Just like your team, this book requires your involvement. You may elect to work through this book with another team member or on your own. As you read each chapter, you'll find concepts and examples from real-team situations. You will also be asked to make choices, judgments, and decisions about team situations. Remember, there are no right or wrong answers in most of these exercises. The idea is to apply basic concepts to various scenarios. In addition, you have the opportunity to do several assignments involving your real team. Finally, to help you remember the salient points, you can use the Checkpoint section at the end of each chapter to crystallize what is most important to you and your team.

SURVIVING IN THE PUSH DOWN WORLD

Teams have a big responsibility, and members of the team carry a piece of the success of the enterprise with them. Despite the central role of teams in all areas of business, industry, higher education, health care, government, and community organizations, many people on teams are never taught the interpersonal and process skills needed to be **team players.** That's what this book is about—giving people who are on teams fundamental skills, tips, and tactics for being good, effective, contributing team players.

As you work through the following chapters, you will be learning how you can contribute to your team as an effective team player. When you complete the exercises and assignments you will be able to:

- Define what a team is and why a team makes sense for your work unit.
- Identify important team player skills and know how to practice them on your team.

- Evaluate how effective your team is, identifying its strengths and weaknesses.
- Influence your team to develop a sound and useful team constitution.
- Contribute your ideas and expertise in solving problems with other team members.
- Help reach agreement and commitment to decisions that result from team discussions.
- Take a role in resolving conflict among team members.
- Anticipate typical barriers to team effectiveness and identify early-warning indicators of these problems in your team.

As you transfer what you learn from this book to real life, you'll find a new level of personal involvement and satisfaction emerging from your work with your team. Working on a truly effective team can have a dramatic positive impact on your own productivity, as well as on your view of work and the people you work with.

Michael D. Maginn

ABOUT THE AUTHOR

Michael D. Maginn is Management Consultant and Senior Vice President of Performance Systems in Boston. He has nearly 20 years of consulting experience in sales and management, quality, leadership, and customer service training, as well as in competency research in many of these areas. The author of several American Management Association video-based training programs in customer service and team building, he was formerly a principal of Singularity Group, Vice President, Research and Development, for the Forum Corporation, and Senior Project Manager of Tratec, Inc. He has been involved in consulting projects for IBM, Chase Manhattan Bank, Harris Bank, Fidelity Investments, Pitney Bowes, PepsiCo, Alcoa Aluminum and Toronto Dominion Bank. Dr. Maginn holds an Ed.D. from the University of Southern California in Educational Psychology and Instructional Technology.

ABOUT
IRWIN PROFESSIONAL
PUBLISHING

Irwin Professional Publishing is the nation's premier publisher of business books. As a Times Mirror company, we work closely with Times Mirror training organizations, including Zenger-Miller, Inc., Learning International, Inc., and Kaset International to serve the training needs of business and industry.

About the Business Skills Express Series

This expanding series of authoritative, concise, and fast-paced books delivers high-quality training on key business topics at a remarkably affordable cost. The series will help managers, supervisors, and frontline personnel in organizations of all sizes and types hone their business skills while enhancing job performance and career satisfaction.

Business Skills Express books are ideal for employee seminars, independent self-study, on-the-job training, and classroom-based instruction. Express books are also convenient-to-use references at work.

CONTENTS

Self-Assessment

Everyone has been on a team of some kind, whether connected with church committees, business projects, sports, or other activities. This self-assessment will highlight areas you may want to focus on as you begin to develop team player skills.

1. T F The three common characteristics of a team are shared goals, people having to work together, and a benefit for everyone.

2. T F The team should get right down to business and start making decisions as soon as it is clear about its goals.

3. T F Laughter and silence are two useful and important aspects of a team that is collaborating to solve a serious business problem.

4. T F A compromise is better than consensus.

5. T F Conflict on teams is beneficial if members understand how to manage it.

6. T F One way to be sure team members arrive at meetings on time is to establish a rule in the team constitution.

7. T F Making announcements is the most effective use of team meeting time.

8. T F When members of a team are committed to a decision, the team has reached a compromise.

9. T F Only the members who know the facts should contribute to the solution.

10. T F A stakeholder is anyone who is affected by the decisions of a team.

Self-Assessment Answers

1. True. A team is any group with common goals, a task that must be done by more than one person, and some kind of payoffs or benefits for every member.

2. False. The team should first develop rules for governing its activities.

3. True. Problem solving and creativity inspire both laughter and thought.

4. False. Members are committed to consensus decisions. Compromise implies some are giving up what they want.

5. True. Differences among members can be channeled and managed to produce high-quality results.

6. True. A team constitution is a set of rules that governs the team's activities.

7. False. Making announcements, although common in team meetings, is not the best use of meeting time.

8. False. A consensus is a decision that team members are committed to.

9. False. Anyone involved on a team or event outside the team can be part of the problem-solving process.

10. True. A stakeholder may not necessarily be on a team but may be impacted by the team's decisions.

1 | What Are Teams All About?

This chapter will help you to:

- Define a team and identify common elements in different kinds of teams.
- Identify why working in a team makes sense in your work.
- Explain what good teams do differently than ineffective teams.
- Explore how team player skills help get things done in a team meeting.
- Examine the set of team player skills you need to be an effective team member.

More organizations of all types and descriptions are creating teams of employees to get things done. Manufacturing firms, insurance companies, banks, research labs, hotels, hospitals and medical centers, service and repair centers, accounting firms, and even restaurants have adopted the team approach, combining the talents of separate individuals into a unified group working cooperatively. Why? The results of effective teamwork are impressive. Research conducted in companies that have switched to a team approach shows that people who work in teams:

- Accomplish more on the job with less waste of time and materials.
- Produce higher-quality work.
- Are happier about their jobs.
- Make customers more satisfied.[1]

---

[1] American Society for Training and Development, Executive Survey on Self-Directed Teams, November 1990.

Working on a team has definite advantages for you as an employee, for your company, and for your customers. Most people have to learn new interpersonal and process skills to become involved, fully effective, and contributing team players.

Technical skills make you successful

Technical skills *plus team player skills* make teamwork successful

Team player skills are different from those you use every day on the technical part of your job, where you normally work on your own. As you will see, team player skills help your team work together effectively. This book should help you take an active role on your team and make a real difference to your work unit and to your organization. Let's start with a look at what teams are.

What Is a Team, Anyway?

Good question. You already know the answer. Think about all the kinds of teams you've ever been on or with which you've been involved. Check all the teams with which you're *personally* familiar.

☐ Sport teams
☐ Fundraising groups
☐ Volunteer organizations
☐ Study groups
☐ Employee committees
☐ Fraternal orders
☐ Political groups
☐ Work committees
☐ Musical groups
☐ School committees
☐ Military units
☐ Work-unit teams
☐ Project teams
☐ Parent-teacher groups

☐ Hobby clubs
☐ Management teams
☐ Cross-functional teams
☐ Problem-solving teams
☐ Church groups
☐ Boy Scout or Girl Scout troops
☐ Quality circles
☐ Boards of directors
☐ Chambers of commerce
☐ Industry associations
☐ Labor union groups
☐ Special-interest groups
☐ Youth groups

Can you think of any other kinds of teams? _____
_____
_____
_____

Whatever the label, committee, group, unit, squad, party, crew, or band, they're all teams. Do you see what all these teams have in common? These groups share the three following characteristics.

Team Characteristic 1: A Shared Purpose or Common Goal.   People with different abilities, talents, experience, and backgrounds have come together for a shared purpose or common goal. Whether making beautiful music, sharing ideas about fly-fishing, planning a business project, or deciding where to hold next year's Christmas party, there is a goal everyone is interested in achieving.

What's the common purpose or goal for a team you are currently involved with?

My team's purpose is: _____

_____

_____

_____

Team Characteristic 2: People Have to Work Together.   All these teams' purposes can't be easily achieved—if at all—by people working by themselves. People need other people to achieve the goal. That's another characteristic of your team.

For example, consider how incredibly difficult it would be to think of new product ideas or design changes in your work unit, and then bring those products or changes into reality by yourself. How hard would it be without the advice, support, and input of other people? Even creative inventors or scientists need other people to put their ideas to work. Other people bring ideas, expertise, experience, resources, and points of view that are different from yours. Different viewpoints and knowledge mean more brainpower is focused on achieving the goal. When all that talent is pooled effectively, no obstacle stands a chance.

Think about the different members on your team. Can you list the unique contribution each person brings to the team?

Team Members	Unique Contribution
_____	_____
_____	_____
_____	_____
_____	_____
_____	_____
_____	_____
_____	_____

Team Members	Unique Contribution

Team Characteristic 3: A Payoff or Benefit for Everyone on the Team.   The work of the team—achieving the purpose or the goal—benefits everyone on the team, directly or indirectly. Perhaps everyone's job becomes easier or more satisfying, the organization improves, or each person simply has fun and learns something in the process. In teams that function well, members quickly see the benefit to themselves, and they become committed to how the team works and the quality of the things the team does.

Not every team starts off with a feeling of commitment. Some people feel skeptical about teams because they've never experienced how satisfying a good team can be when working towards a common goal.

Can you think of the benefit to you if your team works effectively and achieves its goal?

The benefit(s) to me is (are): _____
_____
_____
_____

When you put together the three characteristics of a team, you have a good definition of what a team is.

A team is a group of people working together to reach a goal that they all believe in and that would be difficult, if not impossible, to achieve by people working alone.

ARE TEAMS RIGHT FOR YOUR KIND OF WORK?

Here are some reasons why a team approach makes sense for a work unit or organization. Check all those that apply to your work unit.

☐ Our bosses can't possibly make every decision, although they knock themselves out trying. Work is getting too complex.

- [ ] The people who do the work have expertise and up-to-date knowledge and know-how about how things really should be done.
- [ ] Working as individual contributors has been unproductive, communications haven't been good, and conflicts are starting to affect morale. Work is getting hard to do.
- [ ] There isn't time to wait for someone else to tell us what to do.
- [ ] Most people think they would feel better about work if they had a say in how things get done and if they took responsibility for improving the work product and the work process.

☐ People in different parts of the organization need to talk to each other more frequently. One group doesn't know what the other is doing.

☐ This organization is changing. We've seen quality-improvement programs, management training, reorganization, and new technology. Teams are the next logical step.

☐ The competitive marketplace has sent a message to our management that we need to be more creative, more flexible, and more efficient. The organization is falling behind.

☐ We all know the results of our work could be better. We need to continuously improve quality and reduce cost and waste.

If you're like most people, you've checked at least one, more likely two or more reasons why a team approach makes sense for you and your work unit. Which of the reasons you checked are the most important and convincing to you?

Important reasons why teams make sense to me: _____
_____
_____
_____
_____
_____

Chances are, teams are soon going to make a big difference in how you work and how you feel about work. Most people find that their whole attitude about coming to work changes when they are able to contribute ideas and opinions, to discuss different ways of doing things, and to actually see their team's solutions working effectively. In fact, members of effective teams even start to feel better about themselves because their co-workers and their companies value them in new ways.

One big reason teams make sense is that they give you an opportunity to grow and learn, knowing you have helped make a difference.

GOOD TEAMS AND NOT-SO-GOOD TEAMS

Being on a team doesn't guarantee success. Effective teams take work on every member's part. Everyone has to be a team player. Let's look at what being team players can do for a group of people working together toward a common goal.

Effective teams *do* make a difference in productivity.

You've had experience on teams before. Consider two completely different team experiences you've had. They can be current teams or teams from your past—summer camp, the military, high school, or scouts. Pick one team experience that worked for you, a team that not only accomplished its goal, but did it in a way that left everyone satisfied, even proud of being associated with the team. Pick another team that was a disaster, one you wish you had never joined and that perhaps you even left or from which you resigned. With those two experiences in mind, answer the questions below for each team:

Question	Good Team Experience	Not-So-Good Team Experience
Did members show up on time?		
Did members come prepared?		
Were the meetings organized?		

Question	Good Team Experience	Not-So-Good Team Experience
Did everyone contribute equally?		
Did discussions help the team make decisions?		
What happened when members disagreed?		
Was there more cooperation or more conflict?		
How committed were members to the ideas or decisions made?		
Did people leave feeling good about the team?		
Did members support the team's decisions after the meeting?		

What do you think the difference is between these two teams? You guessed it: individuals were acting like team players. It's not just the team leader. Good team leaders do encourage team members to practice good team player skills, and a person who is not trained to lead a team usually doesn't even give members a chance to be team players. But even the best-trained and most dynamic and fair team leader in the world can't work with a team that is unwilling to contribute, to discuss, and to cooperate.

Even great team leaders can't do team members' work.

So the difference in team effectiveness can often be traced to how the members take responsibility for the work of the team. What really count are the individuals and what they do. How do team members make the difference between good and not-so-good team experiences?

Indicator	Good Team Experience	Not-So-Good Team Experience
Members arrive on time?	Members are prompt because they know others will be	Members drift in sporadically, and some leave early
Members prepared?	Members are prepared and know what to expect	Members are unclear what the agenda is
Meeting organized?	Members follow a planned agenda	The agenda is tossed aside, and freewheeling discussion ensues.
Members contribute equally?	Members give each other a chance to speak; quiet members are encouraged	Some members always dominate the discussion; some are reluctant to speak their minds
Discussions help members make decisions?	Members learn from others' points of view, new facts are discussed, creative ideas evolve, and alternatives emerge	Members reinforce their belief in their own points of view, or their decisions were made long before the meeting
Any disagreement?	Members follow a conflict-resolution process established as part of the team's policies	Conflict turns to argument, angry words, emotion, blaming
More cooperation or more conflict?	Cooperation is clearly an important ingredient	Conflict flares openly, as well as simmering below the surface
Commitment to decisions?	Members reach consensus before leaving	Compromise is the best outcome possible; some members don't care about the result
Member feelings after team decision	Members satisfied, valued for their ideas	Members glad it's over, not sure of results or outcome
Members support decision afterward?	Members are committed to implementation	Some members second-guess or undermine the team's decision

FOUR KINDS OF TEAM PLAYER SKILLS

In an effective team, members act differently than those on a less-effective team. Although many things happen in a team meeting—discussions occur about events and people or what has happened recently or should have happened, opinions are expressed about who should do what, and the like—there are basically four kinds of team player skills that members can use to make a difference and keep their team meetings on track:

1. **Team Constitution.**   Members help develop, follow, and enforce the team's own preestablished policies and procedures—the team's constitution. The effective team develops its own rules about how it will conduct business. These rules range from simple ones, like having members arrive on time and notifying attendees about the agenda, to complex policies, such as how to resolve conflict.

    It is the responsibility of all team members to know and understand these rules and to comply with them for the sake of the team.

2. **Team Collaboration.**   Members work together to discuss ideas and to generate alternative and creative solutions. Team members need to encourage one another to contribute ideas, expand and build on interesting thoughts, and express what is on their minds. When members collaborate on solving a problem, their minds are all working together. The result is often an extraordinarily creative and unique approach to difficult situations.

    It is the responsibility of all team members to make sure that everyone gets a chance to offer ideas—even risky or silly-sounding ideas—without being ridiculed or ignored.

3. **Team Consensus.**   Members make an effort to reach decisions that every team member can support and feel committed to. This not only ensures a team's decisions will be put to work on the job, but it also means members believe the best decision has been made. Consensus is a stronger and more powerful outcome than compromise. A team with consensus is united.

    It is the responsibility of team members to stick with a discussion until all issues are unravelled, consensus among members is formed, and reservations are resolved.

4. **Team Cooperation in Dealing with Conflict.**   Instead of turning a disagreement into an emotional argument, members view conflict as a chance to fully explore issues and differences, to discover new data, and to think about decisions from a number of perspectives. Team members don't hide conflict. The effective team member knows that conflict is natural and that a full, far-reaching, and fact-filled discussion about the conflict will eventually lead members to a clearer understanding of different points of view. Once the underlying problem becomes clear, the resolution is only a few thoughts away.

    It is the responsibility of all team members to approach conflict and disagreement nondefensively and to discuss differences open mindedly. On a team, no one "wins" an argument.

■ Expanding What You Have Learned

Broaden your understanding of teams by answering the following questions:

1. The three characteristics of any team are, (1) common goals, (2) work can't be done alone, and (3) payoff for team members. What would happen if a team lacked one or more of these elements? Picture what a team meeting would be like. Have you ever experienced a similar situation?

_____

_____

_____

2. There are many reasons for using a team approach to achieve a common purpose. Can you think of three reasons why a team approach would not be useful? What kinds of goals might be involved.

_____

_____

_____

3. Team members make the difference in how effective a team is, just like the players on a baseball team win or lose a game. But what about the team leader? If your team is like a sports team, what role should the leader play? What should leaders be sure to do at team meetings? What should they avoid?

_____

_____

_____

4. Of the four team skills, which do you think you carry out well now? Which will you find easy? Which will you find difficult?

_____

_____

_____

5. Of the four team skills, which do you think your team handles well now? Which does the team need to improve?

_____

_____

_____

Chapter Checkpoints

Type of Team Player Skill

✓ Team constitution.

✓ Team collaboration.

✓ Team consensus.

✓ Team cooperation in dealing with conflict.

Individual Responsibility

✓ Establish and enforce the team's own basic rules, policies, and procedures, and comply with them for the sake of the team.

✓ Ensure that unusual, risky, or innovative ideas are offered and developed without negative judgment in a relaxed, enjoyable atmosphere

✓ Encourage decision making based on facts, direct experience, and logic that explores the differences and similarities among team members' points of view

✓ Remain flexible, nondefensive, and open minded when disagreements occur; don't let conflict linger and develop into arguments

2 | Writing the Team Constitution

This chapter will help you to:

- Identify the role of a constitution in making a team work more effectively.
- Examine the kinds of rules teams can make for themselves.
- Develop a draft team constitution.
- Identify ideas from a sample constitution that may be useful to you.
- Find ways that you, as a member, can influence the team to stick by its rules.

The Tale of the Formerly Friendly Tourists

A group of tourists—three married couples from the same home town—arrived in a far-away city. After settling in, they gathered in the hotel lobby to make an important decision—how to spend their day together seeing the sights.

"That's easy," said one. "Let's go to the art museums and then the cathedral."

"Wait a minute, I'd like to go shopping and then go on a bus tour" said another.

"Okay, I've got it," said a third. "The men can go to their museums and restaurants and the women can go shopping." A pause. The idea was an obvious—and uninspiring—solution.

One woman spoke up. "Look, I came here to spend time with my husband. I didn't save up for this vacation to walk around a strange city with women I see every day at home. This was supposed to be our time together. It's important to me."

Three of the six folded their arms, bowing out of the conversation. This was not their idea of a vacation. The remaining three juggled ideas. One finally said, "You know, we've made this too difficult, and we're wasting time. Why don't we all go our separate ways and meet for dinner around 7 P.M.?"

"But people eat dinner here at 9 or 10 at night," said another, with an air of frustration.

"So, I'm still going to be hungry by 6 o'clock," said another, beginning to argue against the local dinner hour custom, explaining in detail the nutritional reasons to eat earlier.

By now, the group was tired of discussing where to go and when to meet for dinner. Some of the members knew the next major decision was going to be what restaurant and what to eat. The thought of another negotiation made everyone tense. After all, this city offered many fine choices.

The couples eventually went their own ways. They went out to dinner and spent time together, but never as a whole group. And, there were strained relations and aggrieved feelings about which couple went to dinner with what other couple. Over the next two weeks, tensions grew. When the tourists went home, they were somewhat disappointed with the vacation, and they silently blamed each other. ∎

Ask yourself:

What went wrong? What would you have done differently?

_____
_____
_____

Have you ever been involved in a situation like this, especially with a new team?

_____
_____

A major mistake that teams make—especially, new teams—is to plunge right into the team's work (like the decision-making discussion the tourists struggled through) before defining a way to work together. If the hapless tourists had spent a few moments deciding how to make the decision they wanted to make they probably would have had a much more successful vacation. At least, they would have remained friends.

Effective teams have a way of avoiding these problems. They take time to decide how to do the things the team has to do—a process called *writing the team's constitution*. Just as the constitution of a country defines how the government will work, a team's constitution establishes operating principles, policies, and ground rules that everyone on the team learns, understands, and is willing to comply with. As the tourists have shown us, if team members don't take time to think through the process of how to work together, conflict soon smolders and then erupts.

2

EXPECTATIONS

Let's imagine you've been selected to be on a work-unit team. You may be pleased, but perhaps, deep down, you feel some reservations.

Can you list any reservations or assumptions you would have about what the team experience will be like?

_____

_____

If you're like most people being asked to be on a work team for the first time, you'll probably feel a little tentative about what will happen on the team and your role on it. Check off any unspoken expressions and assumptions you may have. Be honest in your answers.

- ☐ I'm not going to contribute anything unless someone asks me a direct question.
- ☐ I'm not sure what this team is supposed to do.
- ☐ The loudest voice is going to get his or her way.
- ☐ If I can't bring up whatever is on my mind, I'm not convinced this team is going to work.
- ☐ This team will probably start with a lot of interest and commitment, but by the third or fourth meeting, that will drop off or be gone.
- ☐ One or two people will eventually do all the work. Every group has a couple of workhorses who volunteer for tasks.
- ☐ If all I have to do is talk, that's all right. I'm too busy to do anything else for this team.
- ☐ What will I have to do to get the team doing what I *know* is right?
- ☐ I wonder which person will dominate the discussions?
- ☐ This is going to take a lot of time, in fact, forever.
- ☐ I can miss a couple of meetings. It's okay.
- ☐ When will my commitment to the team end?

Ask yourself what happens to teams if these assumptions and expectations come true in team meetings:

_____

_____

Members bring reservations and assumptions to their new team, and if these feelings are not addressed, they can lead to fragmentation and difficulties in sustaining commitment to the team. Often, these assumptions are based on past experiences with less-effective teams, whose members didn't practice good team skills. A team constitution is designed to clear doubts about what will happen on the team. It creates a positive, specific framework that describes how the team will work—a framework that everyone agrees to follow.

2

HOW DOES THE TEAM WRITE A CONSTITUTION?

The answer depends on the team. Wise leaders will ask the members' help in identifying the kinds of rules that make sense for the team and will then work with the team to develop and document the rules before they are needed. A less desirable procedure is to wait until problems occur, signaling that the team needs policies and standard practices. Next, we'll look at two ways to write a team constitution.

Method One: Future-Forward— The Team Victory Party

One way to approach the task of writing a team constitution is to imagine the future success of the team and work backward from there, defining what it took to get there. Let's say you're starting a major team project. Ask yourself and the other members to imagine that the project has been completed successfully and effectively.

From this future perspective, amidst the (future) good feelings and celebration, look back and ask:

- ☐ What were our meetings like? How were they conducted?
- ☐ How did we reach high-quality decisions?
- ☐ Who was involved and when?
- ☐ What indicators told us we were doing a good job as a team?
- ☐ How did people feel about being on the team? Why did they feel that way?

☐   How were crises and problems handled? What was the atmosphere in the meeting room?

☐   How were differences of opinion handled? How did people feel about discussions?

☐   What role did the team leader play?

Think through the answers to these questions. For example, how did people feel about being on the team? On an effective team that practices good team skills, members will feel valued, glad they have a chance to contribute, and proud to be associated with the group. Now, what did the team do to ensure that people would feel valued? In team meetings, people respected other members' feelings. That's a team rule: Respect the feelings of others.

What indicators told us we were doing a good job as a team? There were probably lots of indicators. We want those that were important to our team. An indicator could be the number of times we sat down and asked ourselves how effective our team was and got any team issues on the table. That's a potential team rule: Sit down regularly and discuss how we're doing.

Take a minute to "think forward" to your team's victory party. Can you list the kinds of rules in your team's constitution that got you there?

_____

_____

_____

_____

Method Two: Anticipating Predictable Problems

Another way to develop a team constitution is to examine the list of predictable and frequent problems any team can expect, especially in its early stages. The team's task is to come up with ideas that avoid these problems—ideas everyone can agree with, ideas that are tailored to your own situation.

Here is a list of some typical team problems. You can probably add your own. See what rules and policies you can put in your constitution to head off these problems before they get in the way of team effectiveness.

- **Predictable Problem: Important People Not Included.**
  Employees who should have been involved with the team from the beginning weren't, leading to problems in selling or implementing the team's decisions. The problem is that the team doesn't discover this omission until important decisions requiring the buy-in of other people have already been made. What rules can be established to make sure that the right people are involved? (Hint: Identify everyone who will be involved with the results or outcomes of the team's work.)

  _____

  _____

- **Predictable Problem: Undisciplined Behavior at Team Meetings.** Members arrive late or not at all. Those who do come are unprepared: some leave early, some get up to take or make phone calls, some read or work on other projects. Noisy private conversations interrupt discussion. Even worse, deadlines and commitments are not met. Apparently, some members don't take the work of the team seriously.

  What rules can be established to ensure the team meetings are disciplined and uphold respect for individuals? (Hint: Are fines for missing start times appropriate? What about a clear statement of expectations?)

  _____

  _____

- **Predictable Problem: Long, Drawn-Out Discussions.** Discussion is central to how a team works. Some lengthy discussions are necessary when making a complex decision. On the other hand, when these discussions are unproductive and rambling, time is wasted, and people become disinterested and eventually agree to anything simply to get out of the meeting. What rules can help keep discussions to the point and productive? (Hint: Consider adopting a discussion format, such as old business, new business, other business or problem statement, ideas, solution choices, and final selection.)

  _____

- **Predictable Problem: Complaining.** Some members think the team meeting is a place to complain about everything they don't like about work. Team meetings encourage participation, but the focus of the team's work is to develop solutions, not to dwell on how individual team members are affected by problems.

What rules can be established to discourage members from using the meeting as their outlet to complain about work or other employees? (Hint: Doesn't every team have a goal? What's your team's goal? Doesn't everyone—even a member with complaints— have positive ideas about how to improve things?)

_____

_____

_____

- **Predictable Problem: The Dominating Team Member.** Every team has one or two members who talk the most or the loudest or who simply don't give other members time to finish what they're saying. While these people may have good ideas, other members don't feel good about the process because discussion seems closed to them.

  What can your team do to control those who tend to dominate discussions, without offending them or turning off their ideas? (Hint: Isn't there a way to encourage equal participation?)

_____

_____

_____

Consider your team and some of the problems you've been facing. Looking over these problems, can you identify some rules that may help avoid or eliminate these problems in the future?

_____

_____

_____

_____

_____

_____

In case you haven't noticed, you've just drafted a team constitution through these different methods. Compare your ideas with the sample team constitution below. Note any ideas you feel will be useful to your own team:

OUR TEAM'S CONSTITUTION

Article One.   We will always be on time for meetings. Right on time. If we must be late or absent, we will inform the team leader or a team member at least a day in advance.

2

Article Two.   We will always come to meetings prepared to work on the agenda that we will receive before the meeting. Our preparation and data collection will be complete, and we will be ready to discuss the issues on the agenda.

Article Three.   We will always respect the opinions and feelings of all individuals. Each member has equal participation in our meetings. When discussing team business, members should expect to contribute to discussions and be listened to with respect.

Article Four.   We will always avoid blaming people for the shortcomings of our team. If our team somehow fails to do its tasks properly, we will examine our team process and attempt to improve it. If individuals are having trouble meeting their commitments, the team will support them in every way possible.

Article Five.   Members will support the decisions of the team after they are made. Undermining team decisions or second-guessing and bad-mouthing the team and its work outside the team setting to nonmembers is *unacceptable* behavior.

Article Six.   Members will live up to their team commitments, recognizing that failure to do so affects the whole team's progress. When in jeopardy of not meeting their obligations, members will notify the team in time for other members to take supportive action.

Article Seven.   When faced with a decision, we will first decide *how* to make the decision. Our general rule is to (1) state the problem, (2) discuss different ideas, (3) examine the benefits and risks associated with different approaches, and (4) select an approach we can all support. Other methods may be appropriate.

Article Eight.   We will deal with conflict in a productive way. Our general rule for conflict is to understand the problem as best we can from each side's perspective. To do that, we will listen to all sides of the conflict, looking for facts and evidence. If there is still a conflict about facts, we will gather additional data. When the problem is understood, the team will help those in conflict create alternative approaches. If misunderstandings are not corrected through this approach, we will call a special meeting to address the conflict.

(continued)

2

Article Nine.   We recognize that working on a team usually results in high-quality ideas and decisions, as well as fun. If we find we are not experiencing these benefits of teamwork, we will pause to assess how we are working together until we better understand our team and our work.

TEN WAYS A TEAM MEMBER CAN INFLUENCE THE TEAM CONSTITUTION

Even if you're not the team leader, you can still play a role in developing and enforcing the team's rules. Check the ideas that make sense to you:

☐ **1.** Ask members if they are satisfied with how the team is operating. Suggest an examination of the team process.

☐ **2.** When a team crisis occurs, take a step back from the problem and examine what kind of problem it is to determine how you can solve it and prevent it from happening again.

☐ **3.** Make sure everyone on the team, especially new members, knows and understands the articles in the team's constitution.

☐ **4.** Diplomatically (and privately) suggest to persistent violators of the constitution that they should examine their degree of commitment to the team.

☐ **5.** Ask other teams how they manage their process, make decisions, and resolve conflict. Use their successful methods for your own team.

☐ **6.** Publicize your team's success, based on the team constitution. Make sure everyone in the organization knows and appreciates the effectiveness of your team's ideas for self-governance.

☐ **7.** Review the constitution before critical meetings that require consensus or collaboration.

☐ **8.** Don't be shy. When you see a violation of the constitution, speak up. It's your team and your constitution.

☐ **9.** Ask the team to form a committee whose goal is to monitor compliance to the constitution.

☐ **10.** Ask the team to review the constitution from time to time to be sure it is still relevant to the work of the team.

■ Expanding What You Have Learned

Use the answers to the following questions to help you and your team prepare to write an effective constitution. Think about these answers by yourself or bring them to a team meeting.

2

1. What kinds of persistent problems is your team experiencing during meetings? Can you trace any of these problems to lack of clear ground rules? What would fix these problems?

_____

_____

_____

2. Team members blame each other for things not done or done incorrectly. How could blaming be avoided by writing clear rules about how the team works together?

_____

_____

_____

3. Does your team meet weekly? Daily? How does the team know it is meeting frequently enough? What kind of problems can be avoided by meeting more frequently?

_____

_____

_____

4. What is your typical agenda? If you had to conduct a meeting in 30 minutes, what would have to change? How about five minutes? What ground rules will help your team conduct a much more efficient meeting in the allotted time?

_____

_____

_____

5. Can you list at least three ideas for orienting new members to how your team works? What are some of the unwritten rules new members should know?

_____

_____

_____

Chapter Checkpoints

Deciding How to Decide

Writing a constitution is one of the most important activities a team can engage in, especially newly formed teams. Keep in mind the following checkpoints that every team should follow:

- ✓ Take the time to decide on operational procedures.
- ✓ Create a constitution that clearly defines the team's rules and policies.
- ✓ Imagine the future success of your team and speculate on what it might take to reach that success.
- ✓ Anticipate problems to formulate solutions *before* the problems occur.
- ✓ Recognize when team rules need to be created, reviewed, and enforced.

3 | How to Get Ideas on the Table

This chapter will help you to:

- Learn what team collaboration is.
- Identify what helps and hinders the creative process.
- List the actions a team member can use in collaborating with others.
- Apply team collaboration skills to different problems.

The Problem with the 1500-B Form

Work Team: Arthur, Beverly, Carlos, Diane

Problem: Customers send in an order form, 1500-B, for processing before a product can be sent to them. Many customers are unhappy because of the delays in getting the product and mistakes in processing. The problem is that the forms are not completed correctly: they are filled with errors and omissions.

How the Team Solved the Problem

Arthur

These order forms are starting to give us more problems than anyone expected.

Beverly

People don't fill them out properly. I can't believe how much information is missing. It slows down the whole process of getting product out to these people.

Carlos

Much too long. A person who sends in an order doesn't get the product for almost four weeks. That's a long time without hearing from us.

Diane

We could send them an acknowledgment.

Beverly

That's a good idea, kind of friendly.

Carlos

Like, "Thanks for sending your application. You'll hear from us, we'll be back to you soon."

Arthur

Yeah, because it'll take three more weeks for us to figure out your handwriting.

[Laughter]

Beverly

Or maybe we'll include an eraser in the envelope.

[More laughter]

Beverly

We *need* that information to process the order. We can't process orders without that information.

Arthur

But a lot of forms come in with information missing all the time. We're experiencing a 35 percent completion rate. If it's not missing, the information customers provide is just wrong.

Diane

I wish people were more organized.

[Pause and silence]

Carlos

This would be a great process if it weren't for the people.

[Laughter, then silence]

Carlos

Maybe people aren't the whole problem.

Arthur

What about changing the form . . . more instructions, bigger type, easier to read.

Beverly

I like that. Change the form.

Carlos

We'll never change people, so we'll change the form.

[Discussion follows about different graphic approaches—larger type, bigger boxes, arrows pointing to examples, and so forth. They redesign the form with a different graphic look.]

Arthur

That'll help, but will it solve the problem?

Diane

We're still going to ask people for information that's not easy to find.

[Pause]

Diane

Maybe we're asking people to provide too much information. Maybe that's the message in all this. Should we think about shrinking the form?

Carlos

Shrinking . . . Hmm, yeah . . . I see what you mean. Let's take another look at that form.

[The team examines the form. They identify 23 separate items for the customer to fill in.]

Beverly

Of the 23 items, I could answer maybe 6 off the top of my head. I'd have to look this other stuff up.

Diane

Like how many cars I ever owned.

Carlos

And my passport number.

Arthur

Passport number? Do we really need that?

Beverly

It used to be important, but not any more. We could eliminate that. A lot of this isn't important anymore.

[The team examined the form and questioned the need for eight items, classifying them as not needed or not critical. They decided another 10 items were good to have, but thought they could gather this information *after* the order was processed, as part of the normal product introduction. Only five items were viewed as critical for processing a new form. They redesigned the form a second time; this version contained only five items.]

Carlos

This will speed up the processing. And it'll allow us to be more competitive. Nice job, team.

Beverly

I think I owned six cars. Or was it five. . . . ■

Judging from how they solved the form problem, would you like to work on this team? Why?

_____

_____

_____

Solving a problem as a group is different from solving a problem as an individual. The team has the power of different ideas and points of view. When team members collaborate effectively, ideas from different people produce creative alternatives and unique approaches to stubborn problems.

What's it like to work on a team that enjoys creating as many alternative solutions as possible? It's fun! That's why team collaboration is the most playful and creative team skill. In this chapter, we'll explore how team members can open the door to solving problems together.

A COLLABORATION SAMPLER

Try this exercise by yourself.

Take 60 seconds to list as many uses for a marshmallow as you can. Have fun, be unorthodox. Write in the spaces below:

_____

_____

_____

How many? Now, ask three other people to list as many uses for a marshmallow as the group can in 60 seconds. Add their uses for a marshmallow:

_____

_____

_____

As you can see, it's more fun and productive to do these tasks in teams. Not only are there more ideas, some of them are really bizarre. You see, teamwork has a distinct advantage. A team has the wisdom, experience, diversity, and creativity of its members. Once a team has a clear and useful constitution as a foundation, they can collaborate on addressing problems.

What emerges from team collaboration? Insightful, perhaps even startlingly high-quality ideas and decisions to improve work, to design new products or services, or simply to remove stubborn problems that get in the way of work.

The key to collaboration is to open the door to ideas, and team members have that key in their possession. Members have a responsibility to create an environment in which ideas can be discussed freely. Teams that collaborate well allow members to have wild and crazy ideas—or at least different and unusual ideas—with no threat of embarrassment or disapproval. Team members build on each other's ideas, modifying them, dropping them, picking them up again—a volleyball game of thoughts.

What Slows Down Collaboration?

People have good ideas, sometimes creative and unusual ideas, all the time. Yes, you're creative. You may not think so, but everyone is. Creativity doesn't only mean being artistic or expressive. We learn as children to play in imaginary worlds where ideas flow and anything is possible. When we grow up, we learn to keep these ideas and images inside. Our thoughts often go unexpressed, especially in team settings. Somewhere in our growing up, we learn to become sensitive—sometimes overly sensitive—to what other people think of our ideas. We are afraid that ideas that were once playful and full of potential might be viewed by others as silly and unbusinesslike.

Paradoxically, organizations need ideas that are different. Where would the great inventions and innovations of today be if the ideas behind them had been put down when they were first expressed? Isn't it silly to think of delivering packages and small parcels overnight by using a huge fleet of airplanes and trucks? Ten years ago, wasn't it comical to think of sending letters over the telephone? Or having upwards of 100 channels on your television? Can you think of other everyday inventions that were developed from different, innovative ideas?

_____

_____

_____

The name of the collaboration game is to break down barriers to creativity and let ideas flow, knocking them around until something wonderful happens— a really GOOD idea is born.

Sure, credit cards, self-service gas stations, telephone answering machines, personal phone numbers, mail-order flowers, television remote controls, hand-held navigation instruments, corporate day care centers, frequent flyer clubs, the list goes on. Even more ideas would come to light with a supportive atmosphere.

Imagine the first meeting in which someone said, "Let's give free flights to people who travel a lot." That team must have been fun. But it's not that simple. It's too easy to stop ideas cold.

How to Stop Ideas Cold

Check off the expressions you've heard in team meetings. How do you think the member offering the idea felt?

- ☐ We tried that already, and it didn't work.
- ☐ Are you serious? Come on!
- ☐ Are you kidding? Come on!
- ☐ They'll never buy that.
- ☐ That's not what we had in mind. (Someone has a preconceived idea of the solution.)
- ☐ Nice thought. Any other ideas? (Whoops, your idea got swept away.)
- ☐ I'm not sure you know enough about it. (Ideas are limited to areas of expertise.)
- ☐ _____ Silence and serious looks.
- ☐ You're not suggesting we do that, are you?
- ☐ We'll never make it work.
- ☐ It won't last.
- ☐ It'll cost too much.
- ☐ Can't we be logical?
- ☐ Yes, but . . . .

How to Bring Ideas to Life

Team members can control the creative atmosphere in meetings. When members practice collaboration skills, everyone is encouraged to offer suggestions. The more suggestions, the more likely the team will come up with new and effective approaches to stubborn problems.

TEAM COLLABORATION SKILLS

What to Do	How to Do It
1. Listen with interest and respect to what members say.	Use body-language (lean forward, nod, take notes). Demonstrate active listening skills (say, "Uh-huh, I see," and repeat important phrases) to let members know you're tuned in and attentive. Allow members to complete their statements without interruption or distractions.

(continued)

3

TEAM COLLABORATION SKILLS (concluded)

What to Do	How to Do It
2. Pursue what is interesting about unique and different ideas.	Find the best characteristic of the idea being offered. For example, "Reducing the amount of information on the form is really interesting." Build on ideas by repeating the unique characteristic and support or expand it. "Less information means a person would complete the form right away from memory." Encourage the member offering the idea to keep explaining what's on his/her mind. "Stick with it, Joan. Tell us more." Ask follow-up questions.
3. Acknowledge and record every idea as it comes up.	Use a flipchart or chalkboard to list ideas. All team members should acknowledge contributions. "Way to go, Harry! Nice idea."
4. Ask others to go beyond the obvious.	Encourage team members to stretch their imaginations. "Come on, team, we need a breakthrough idea." Ask the team to do a loosening up exercise, like collecting uses for a marshmallow. Give people permission to be creative. Remember, the first solution is not necessarily the best solution.
5. Collect a *quantity* of ideas. Quality will soon become evident.	Ask members to state as many ideas as possible. The team will have time to refine them later. Keep asking, "Any other ideas?" and wait until they emerge. Stick with it. Don't be discouraged if ideas develop slowly.
6. Allow time for thinking.	Don't confuse silence with inattentiveness. Silence is the sound of thinking. Change the meeting location. Take a break or a walk. Come back tomorrow. Change the subject. Ignore periods of confusion and frustration. They're natural.
7. Ask critics for ideas and suggestions.	If someone criticizes an idea, ask him or her to offer a new idea in its place or build on the idea in question.
8. Encourage people to ask "what-if" questions.	Use a metaphor. "What if our application form were on a post card. What information would we ask for?" Remove constraints. "What if we did have more time to solve this problem. What would the solution look like?" Change perceptions. "What if Frank Sinatra were solving this problem. What would he say?" Draw the problem as a picture.
9. Avoid criticism and judgment of ideas.	Advise naysayers about the team constitution. Treat all ideas equally as they are expressed. Reward people for their contributions.
10. Have fun.	Order a pizza. Wear casual clothes, sit on the floor, close the door, play music, tell jokes. Give everyone a kazoo. (It's been done in the best of organizations!)

Which of these skills is your team already fairly good at?

_____
_____
_____
_____

Which need improvement?

_____
_____
_____
_____

3

Team Collaboration Exercises: Get Ready for Creativity

Select some problems to solve. You'll need to find at least two friends to help develop ideas. Before you begin, select two or three team collaboration skills to practice during the exercise. Watch the interaction among team members as you develop your ideas.

1. On a flipchart, draw a new logo for your organization. Make sure it reflects what people really value and think.

2. Can you identify 100 no-cost ways to improve quality in your work unit? How about 50?

3. Imagine your team has invented a machine that reverses the pull of gravity and can be attached to anything that is not living. Develop an illustrated consumer-magazine advertisement for the product including (a) its name, (b) slogan, (c) features and benefits. Draw your ad on a flipchart.

4. Remember the Mona Lisa, one of Leonardo da Vinci's masterpieces? Can you and your friends explain the real story behind that smiling face? Write down all the possible explanations.

5. Gather some old magazines and cut out pictures. A medium-sized stack will do. Now, with your friends, put the pictures together in a sequence to tell a story that somehow ends with you and your friends. When you're ready, tell the story to your team or your family.

Tips for Improving Team Collaboration Skills

If you and team or family members worked through some of these exercises and applied the team collaboration skills, you probably laughed a lot and created more interesting results than you could have by yourself. Here are some additional suggestions for making team collaboration work. Check those that you want to take back to your team:

☐ Practice, practice, practice is certainly the best way to improve team members' collaboration skills. With practice, these skills are not difficult.

☐ Conduct creative warm-up exercises at every team meeting. The members will soon get the idea that problem-solving is fun.

☐ Interestingly, most people need permission to let their ideas out. Tell them it's okay to offer interesting ideas, even unorthodox ideas.

☐ Post team collaboration skills on the wall and review them before the next meeting.

☐ Allow time for ideas to happen. Sometimes focusing on coming up with a neat idea in only one meeting works. The urgency of a deadline makes some team members inventive and resourceful. At other times, a problem can be so difficult or complex that original thoughts need to incubate, perhaps over a few hours or overnight. When members' enthusiasm for problem-solving seems to flag, the team should take a break.

☐ Suggest that your team visit other teams that are good at collaboration skills. Ask members to come to your meetings. Compare the creative process in both groups and learn from each other.

☐ Get an outside facilitator to attend your meetings. Having an outsider act as a referee and facilitator is a highly effective way to explode the barriers to creativity on your team.

☐ Ask your team to practice "ambiance engineering." Change the meeting room around. Move the furniture, meet in the company cafeteria, meet off site, meet outside, wear different clothes, wear costumes, give out toys, play a game, and do the unexpected.

☐ Go to school on the problem. Do some action research. Visit the problem where it happens. Observe how the problem occurs, talk to the people actually involved, perform any tasks or operations yourself, experience what it's like to be a customer or the recipient of the problem.

☐ Celebrate an exciting and productive team meeting with a fun event. Go to a movie or on a boat ride. Show a Charlie Chaplin movie.

☐ Think of some respected and credible figure in the company, the person who has the best reputation for creativity, ideas, and uniqueness. Ask the team to think about how that person would address the problem.

Expanding What You Have Learned

Here are some thought-provoking questions about team collaboration skills.

1. How can you tell when collaboration is working effectively? What does it feel like?

_____

_____

_____

2. When are obvious solutions most likely to appear? Why is it important to search beyond the obvious solution?

_____

_____

_____

3. Examine your team's climate for creativity. What creative ideas do you, as a team member, have for improving the environment for collaboration?

_____

_____

_____

4. Imagine where your team will be when every member contributes freely and feels safe about saying what is on his or her mind. What kind of things will your team be able to do then that it has trouble doing now?

_____

_____

_____

5. Suspending judgment when listening to ideas can be difficult. What rules can you ask the team to insert in the team constitution that will help members listen without criticizing?

_____

_____
_____

_____

Chapter Checkpoints

Collaboration Means Permission to Be Creative

Of all the team skills, collaboration is clearly the most fun. When members collaborate, they identify innovative and ingenious ways to solve problems. Remember:

✓ Everyone can be creative—don't allow your preconceptions to color your view of teammates' capabilities.

✓ Give permission to everybody to be creative in an effort to solve problems.

✓ Allow plenty of time for idea development.

✓ Never dismiss an idea for seeming silly or frivolous. These are opportunities to develop new approaches.

✓ Listen to all ideas.

✓ Encourage teammates to play with concepts and ideas even before a serious idea emerges.

✓ Perhaps break up heavy sessions with less serious activities to ease tension and change the pace.

✓ After a tension-reducing break, go back to the problem with renewed energy.

4 | Decisions the Team Can Stand Behind

This chapter will help you to:

- Distinguish between consensus and compromise.
- Learn the benefits of consensus in team decision making.
- Identify the kinds of decisions that will benefit from decision making by consensus.
- Identify the team consensus skills you can use in your team.
- Apply team consensus skills in an exercise.

Problem: Five team members have to agree on selecting a new member. Before they discuss the candidates, they decide to identify the selection criteria. They agree on three qualities the new member should have—technical expertise, willingness to participate, and cooperativeness. They are having trouble deciding on the fourth, and final, criterion.

"I say it's loyalty," said the first member. "If people aren't loyal to the team, they can undo all our decisions after we make them."

The second member responded, "Loyalty? Isn't that a bit old fashioned. It sounds like conformity to me. We need people who can think independently and have ideas, not loyal dull heads."

The first member replied, "Who says people who are loyal have to be dull or nonthinking?"

"Well, that's what comes to my mind," the second member rejoined.

The discussion went around the table. The other members gave their views of loyalty. To one, loyalty meant standing up for the team whenever it was challenged by others, defending its decisions. To another, loyalty meant following the team's constitution and being a team player—sticking to the rules and doing an equal share. To the next person, loyalty was more practical.

"To me, loyalty means agreeing to follow the team's direction, even though you originally thought it was incorrect."

"Well," said the first team member, "I guess that really focuses the difference on me. My idea of loyalty—being a conformist—doesn't seem to be the same as you two think. I think a person who is loyal is a good soldier, someone who does what is told."

The team discussed these differences. The member who had viewed loyalty as conformity agreed that the others' ideas made sense, but he still had trouble with the word loyalty.

"If loyalty means different things to this group, it'll have all kinds of different meanings to our candidates," he said.

The team agreed on the term *team player* to incorporate all their thoughts about loyalty, and each one felt committed to the decision.

The four selection criteria were then used to identify many excellent candidates. The next consensus the group faced was selecting the candidate who best matched the criteria. It was difficult, but they emerged with a person they all agreed on. And they all felt she was the right choice. ■

Let's take a look at this situation. What does the word *loyalty* mean to you? What would you have said in the team meeting? Would you have agreed with the consensus? Think it over:

_____

_____

_____

This team reached consensus by exchanging views about the meaning of a particular word. When each member expressed what the word meant to him or her, the team was able to see similarities and differences. When members discussed differences in an open-minded way, the team was able to agree on what they *really* meant. The team came to a decision they could all stand behind.

We're going to explore the concept of *team consensus* and what you, as a member, can do to influence consensus decisions on a team.

COMPROMISE VERSUS CONSENSUS

You and some friends are going to rent a movie one evening. Everyone wants a different one. Some of the group—but not you—feel rather strongly about certain films and movie stars. Do you:

1. Dig your heels in and defend your choice?
2. Pick up a book and read in another room?
3. Go along with what people want?

In that kind of situation, you would probably just go along with whatever movie was selected. You didn't care that much about the movie anyway and, well, it's probably more important and fun just being with your friends than winning the movie argument. This is an example of a compromise decision. What words do you associate with compromise? What about the consequences of a compromise decision?

_____

_____

_____

A compromise is a way of getting a decision people can live with. Generally, the result is all right, but not terrific. Some words that you might associate with a compromise might be, *half-hearted, reluctant, settlement, concession,* or *arrangement.* Some people say that a camel is an animal designed by the compromises of a committee.

Certainly, compromises are important and expedient answers to some problems. The problem with a compromise is that the outcome doesn't meet everyone's expectations. In fact, there may be some winners and losers in a compromise decision. When people make a decision they are not 100 percent committed to, they may feel half-hearted and reluctant about putting that decision into action.

Can you think of any decisions your team may have made that were compromises? How did members feel about this? Write a description of your reaction to a real compromise decision:

_____

_____

_____

_____

_____

_____

_____

_____

Consensus—Making Lasting Decisions

Your work team has been asked to decide if the company should adopt flexible work-hour scheduling. Employees would have to work 40 hours a week, but individuals could work four 10-hour days, or one 12-hour day and four 7-hour days, or other combinations of time, as long as it resulted in a full 40 hours. As you can see, there are some obvious advantages as well as disadvantages. Management needs your team's decision in two hours. Do you:

1. Fold your arms and watch the argument unfold?
2. Argue forcefully for your optimal time slot?
3. Discuss what people think and see how the group feels?
4. Decide the decision is too complex to make, so you recommend saying no to flexible scheduling.

Opting out of making decisions because they appear complex or difficult only means that opportunities for improving work and the quality of work life will slip by or, even worse, be made by someone else. Arguing on the basis of self-interest will only lead to more arguing, delaying a decision until individuals are worn down and willing to compromise, and you now know where that leads.

This decision requires a group commitment. That kind of agreement is called a consensus. Basically, the process of achieving consensus involves getting people with different points of view to start seeing things in a similar way or at least narrowing their differences.

Different points of view of the same experience
get in the way of consensus.

An Anecdote: The King, the Three Wise People, and the Mysterious Animal

A rich king was intrigued by reports of an unusual animal who lived far across the sea. He decided to send his three brightest and wisest scholars to visit the animal and bring back a description. The three traveled to the far-off land, finally arriving at night at the edge of a dense jungle, where they heard the animal thrashing around in a grove of trees. In the pitch-black darkness, each of the wise people—quite afraid by now—walked into the grove to touch the animal. One by one they emerged, and they quickly departed to report to the king.

(continued)

(concluded)

Back at the castle, the king asked eagerly, "What is this animal like? "Why, it had a great side as far up as I could reach," said the first wise person. "No, it was thin and had a hairy head," said the second. "No, no, it had a thick round neck," said the third. The three began arguing about what the animal was like. Each had touched the same animal, but how could they see it so differently? The king, thinking of the expense of sending three so-called wise people on such a long trip, had them all thrown into the dungeon. He still didn't know what the mysterious animal looked like.

Unfortunately, the wise people never shared their points of view, their perceptions. To each one, his or her own view of the elephant was the only correct one.

In a consensus, the various points of view of each member of the team are considered, discussed, compared, and discussed again until everyone sees *all* parts of the elephant. Members begin to learn about others' perceptions, and a decision or approach emerges as differences are understood and narrowed. This outcome goes beyond something people can go along with. Instead, it is a decision team members believe in as the truly best way to go, given the circumstances. Because the issue has been examined, reexamined, tested through discussion, critiqued, and poked, and prodded, all members of the team can see the problem and the solutions from many different points of view.

One of the major benefits of a consensus decision is that it brings team members, who start off with differing points of view, to a common understanding of all the issues. In a way, it's a learning experience. Members learn how others see their part of the elephant. Through discussion of how fellow members see the problem, everyone begins to share perceptions. Differences don't appear as great as they once did.

Building a Shared View—10 Team Consensus Skills

Team members can practice consensus skills any time the group needs to reach a decision that everyone must buy into. When the decision is actually implemented in the work unit, people support it and the desired results start to happen. The table shows ways to narrow differences in points of view among team members.

What to Do	How to Do It
1. Ask each individual how he or she feels about the situation and why.	Go around the table, and give everyone his or her say. "How do you see this problem, Dave?" Stop team members who are dominating discussion, and poll everyone else. Ask members who are silent what they think.
2. Ask for facts, definitions, or explanations, and try to uncover what different thoughts or words *really* mean to team members.	Ask members to explain their views. Focus on words. For instance, "What does *loyalty* mean to you?" or "What's a *significant* delay?" Ask, "How do you know that?" when faced with questionable statements.
3. Clarify discrepancies of opinion with facts.	State facts and ask other team members to compare opinions with the facts. Ask members to support competing points of view with facts. If there are no available facts, ask members to gather data before continuing.
4. Modify your views when faced with compelling facts and opinions.	Listen to the facts underlying differing points of view. Test the facts being presented against your viewpoint. Weigh the impact on you and the team of continuing to resist ideas in the face of convincing facts. Try on the other point of view and see how it feels. Is it really that different from yours? Are the consequences acceptable?
5. Identify similarities and differences among the points of view in the team.	Make a list of similarities and differences on a flipchart or chalkboard. Ask different members to state what is similar about their ideas. Crystallize the difference among team members in a simple statement, "It seems some people view centralization as a threat, while others see it as an opportunity."
6. Reinforce openmindedness—that is, the willingness to listen to other views—and the need for cooperation.	Remind members about the team constitution's rules concerning open discussion. Give people time to talk. Make sure they have said what is on their minds. Review the team's goal from time to time, and stress the need to work together to come to agreement.
7. Remain nondefensive when challenged and avoid emotional encounters.	Stay silent and calm when being criticized. Wait until the other member has finished before commenting. Take notes reflecting the other member's points. Summarize the other member's opinion in your own words. If the meeting is getting emotional, ask for a short recess, take a walk, try to relax. Be empathic with other's views. Say, "I can understand why you would say that."
8. List the positive and negative aspects or consequences of each point of view.	Assume the team has adopted a particular viewpoint. Ask members to discuss the advantages and disadvantages. Repeat the process with the next opinion. Explore the risks associated with each idea. Test how realistic different people's assessment of the risks are. "Will we really have *significant* delays in meeting customer orders?"
9. Be sure that each team member participates.	Go around the table and ask all the members what they think. "What do you think loyalty means?" Members have a responsibility to speak their minds.

(continued)

4

What to Do	How to Do It
10. Through discussion, define the level of risk associated with a decision and develop an approach that minimizes that risk for everyone.	Ask people what concerns them about a specific course of action. "What do you think will happen if we go to flexible scheduling?" If concerns are based on a misperception or misunderstanding, explain the facts. "Alice, the system is voluntary, not mandatory. Does that help?" Balance the advantages and risks of each approach. Ask the team what level of risk it is willing to accept.

TEAM ASSESSMENT

Before going on, ask yourself how well your team practices these consensus skills. Rate each skill from 1 to 10 according to the scale. Identify which skills need improvement and, in the space provided, list some ideas for improving that skill among your team members.

Do We:	Rarely			Sometimes				Always		
1. Ask each individual how he or she feels about the situation and why?	1	2	3	4	5	6	7	8	9	10
2. Ask for facts or explanations, and try to uncover what different thoughts or words mean to everyone?	1	2	3	4	5	6	7	8	9	10
3. Clarify discrepancies of opinion with facts?	1	2	3	4	5	6	7	8	9	10
4. Modify our views when faced with compelling facts and opinions?	1	2	3	4	5	6	7	8	9	10
5. Identify similarities and differences among the points of view in the team?	1	2	3	4	5	6	7	8	9	10
6. Reinforce open-mindedness—the willingness to listen to other views—and the need for cooperation?	1	2	3	4	5	6	7	8	9	10
7. Remain nondefensive when challenged, and avoid emotional encounters?	1	2	3	4	5	6	7	8	9	10
8. List the positive and negative aspects or consequences of each point of view?	1	2	3	4	5	6	7	8	9	10
9. Make sure that each team member participates?	1	2	3	4	5	6	7	8	9	10
10. Define the level of risk associated with a decision, and develop an approach that minimizes that risk for everyone?	1	2	3	4	5	6	7	8	9	10

What are your three highest-rated skills? What are members doing in team meetings to earn that score?

Three Highest-Rated Skills	Actions
_____	_____
_____	_____
_____	_____

Now, identify the three lowest-rated skills. Identify things you and your team can do to improve these consensus skills. Refer to the "How to Do It" suggestions.

Three Lowest-Rated Skills	Improvement Ideas
_____	_____
_____	_____
_____	_____

TEAM CONSENSUS EXERCISES— JUST DOING IT

One way to help your team improve is to work together on a nonwork-related problem. While the team is working through the following exercises, each member should try to concentrate on practicing at least one of the team consensus skills. After the exercise is over, ask the team to reflect on how the consensus process went and how well the team consensus skills were applied. Here are several exercises from which to choose.

Team Consensus Exercise 1—Scoring Your Team's Consensus Skills (Estimated time: 30 minutes). Review the list of team consensus skills with your team. First, each member is to rate each skill individually. When everyone is finished, compare the individual rating and come to agreement on a group rating for each skill. This will require all team members to explain why they gave the ratings they did. Remember, each team member has to select at least one team consensus skill before you begin and actively try to practice it during the exercise. After the group has completed the exercise, see how the members felt about the consensus process. Finally, compare this exercise with what really goes on in team meetings.

Team Consensus Exercise 2—Lively Discussions on Hot Topics (Estimated time: 30–60 minutes). In this exercise, your team can address several interesting and controversial issues. The idea is for the team to come to a consensus on how it feels. Once again, ask each team member to select a team consensus skill and apply it during the exercise. Here are some issues to discuss. Select one you think would lead to a lively discussion.

1. Vehicular traffic in cities should be limited to delivery trucks and taxis during work hours.
2. Children should be required to do at least an hour of homework every night.
3. Television programs showing violence should be shown only after 9 P.M..
4. Surplus military clothing should be given to the homeless.
5. All students must demonstrate fluency in at least two languages to graduate college.
6. Schools should operate year-round, with summer outdoor programs appropriate to the locality.
7. Salary increases of team members should reflect the success of the team, not individuals.

Team Consensus Exercise 3—The Excellent Team Member (Estimated time: 45 minutes). Have your team review the following list of 20 descriptive words. Each team member is to select only five words which, according to him or her, describe the most important characteristics of a team member. After members have made their individual choices, the team has to arrive at a consensus on the five most important characteristics of a team member. Which five descriptors will the team choose? Before the team discusses the characteristics, ask each member to select a team consensus skill to apply in the consensus process. Don't vote. Discuss. There are no right or wrong answers to this exercise.

Characteristics of the Excellent Team Member

1. Vocal.	6. Motivated.	11. Well-read.	16. Efficient.
2. Experienced.	7. Respected.	12. Good thinker.	17. A leader.
3. Lively.	8. Sensitive.	13. Helpful.	18. People-person.
4. Ambitious.	9. Interesting.	14. Expert.	19. Energetic.
5. Risk-taker.	10. Willing.	15. Good networker.	20. Well known.

■ Expanding What You Have Learned

Broaden your understanding by asking yourself the following questions:

1. Consensus is the agreement and commitment of the team to an idea or decision. How do you know the team has reached a consensus? What can you do to make sure the team has really come to agreement?

_____

_____

_____

2. Remaining nondefensive when other team members are critical of your views is often difficult. Can you think of at least two reasons why you might get defensive when your ideas are challenged? How does understanding the reasons for getting defensive help you deal with criticism?

_____

_____

_____

3. Why is it important not to vote to reach consensus? In your team, when do you think voting is a good alternative to consensus for making a team decision?

_____

_____

_____

4. Review your team constitution. Are ground rules included to help the team in consensus discussions? Should you try to regulate arguments, limit discussion time or language?

_____

_____

_____

5. Open-mindedness is an important aspect of consensus. Think about something you believe in strongly. Tell yourself you're willing to really listen to other viewpoints. What, if anything, would it take to get you to change your mind? What about other issues? Are there different criteria that would make you flexible? What does it take to make you open-minded?

_____

_____

_____

Chapter Checkpoints

Sharing Perceptions, Gaining Commitment

Consensus building is one of the most powerful team player skills. Members who understand how to reach consensus find that decisions are implemented as planned. Members believe in the group's decision because they've had an active part in examining a problem and determining its solution. Remember:

✓ Beware of compromises—not everyone is wholeheartedly behind an idea.

✓ Reaching consensus guards against later I-told-you-so comments from disgruntled teammates.

✓ Take time for everyone to share perceptions about the problem.

✓ Ensure that everyone gets a chance to share initial viewpoints before proceeding to identify areas of agreement.

✓ Encourage all team players to keep a flexible point of view.

✓ Exchange ideas—this is a great way to learn.

✓ Keep an open, nondefensive mind.

CHAPTER

5 | Learning to Manage Conflict

This chapter will help you to:

- Recognize typical sources of conflict in work teams.
- Describe five methods for dealing with conflicting ideas and approaches.
- Identify things to do to build trust among team members so that conflict becomes an asset, not a destructive force.

Conflict. The word conjures up images for everyone. What do you think of when you think of the word *conflict*? Write three images that come to mind:

_____
_____
_____

Let's examine this topic a little more closely. Conflict. Say you're in a team meeting, presenting your ideas. You think you've been pretty smart, even brilliant. Then, someone says, "I don't agree. I don't think we should do that at all. In fact, we ought to do it this way." How do you feel? Write what best describes your feelings at that moment:

_____
_____
_____

Conflict touches everyone. There is no escaping it. As you probably indicated, conflict is usually not a positive experience. It isn't for most people. In fact, conflict makes some people so uncomfortable that they would do anything to avoid it. That's because conflict between people often makes its appearance through angry words, pounding fists, emotional and loud voices, hurt feelings, withdrawal, and even confusion. Ideas stop flowing, people stop talking, things stop happening.

It doesn't have to be that way. In teams, conflict comes with the territory. Whenever a diverse group of people come together to work as a team toward a common goal, their ideas about how to get things done are going to be different. There will be conflict. Successful team members recognize the value of bringing different opinions to the table, and they manage the resulting conflict.

Expect team members to bring their unique opinions to the team. Manage the differences, don't let conflict become "personal".

Instead of stirring up anger and emotion, conflict becomes an opportunity. When teams understand how to make conflict an opportunity, conflict doesn't stop work. Instead, it actually energizes work. As you'll see, it takes cooperation and trust among team members to harness that energy and put conflict to work.

AVOIDING UNNECESSARY CONFLICT

Effective team members are not afraid of conflicting ideas. In fact, conflicting ideas forge higher-quality outcomes. Some team conflicts are valuable. On the other hand, every team member should be wary of unnecessary conflict. Unnecessary conflict gets in the way of the team's work.

Look at the following list of the typical sources of conflict for a team. Can you identify which sources might be valuable and which ones unnecessary and suggest how to avoid an unnecessary source of conflict?

Typical Source of Conflict	Valuable or Unnecessary?	If Unnecessary, How to Avoid?
1. Goals and rewards differ among team members. Self-interest predominates.		
2. Members view the business from their own functional view (e.g., finance, operations, sales), without seeing the big picture.		
3. Members haven't been told to cooperate, or they believe that the team is a chance to win while others lose.		
4. New members join the team late and bring up ideas already addressed by the team.		
5. Members think they are right because they have facts or experience other team members don't have.		
6. Members like to test ideas by challenging decisions and authority.		
7. Some members have values and beliefs about work that sometimes are contrary to the group.		

See if you agree with these sources of conflict.

Goals and Rewards Are Different.   Unfortunately, many teams are formed by individuals whose "real" work is not the team's work. One of the fundamental and defining characteristics of teams—a common goal and benefits for all—is missing. This source of conflict is unnecessary. Team members, even those from different parts of an organization, should be accountable for their team work and should be rewarded for its success. Team rewards are common in many organizations that empower groups of workers. These issues may be addressed through the team constitution.

Functional Views of the Business Prevail.   While you might say it is valuable to have differing views around the team table, if there is not a shared common view of how all the pieces of the business fit together as a system, the resulting conflict can be unproductive. Too often, different functions within an organization come to a team to represent their own

5

interests. A team can avoid this unnecessary conflict by developing a systems diagram—a map—of how each function contributes and is linked to serving the customer. This is an important ground rule to establish *before* team work can be effective.

People Want to Win.   Long-established rivalries among people, departments, and locations can cause members to arrive at team meetings with a fear that another member may gain something—extra resources, power, prestige, access to higher levels—at his or her expense. As a result, team meetings run into unnecessary roadblocks. Politics is a reality in businesses. A well-thought-out team constitution may go a long way in breaking down these barriers.

New Members Join the Team Late.   New members should be briefed and thoroughly oriented to the team, its goals, the team constitution, the history of its achievements, its strengths and future plans. New members can also be assigned a mentor to assist in their orientation process. In this way, unnecessary conflict can be avoided. On the other hand, revisiting ideas through the naive questions and ideas of new members may be a valuable way to review how decisions were made. New members may even contribute a fresh perspective and surprising insights to problems the group thought it had addressed completely.

Members Think They Are Right.   Facts, opinions, and experience are the currency of team meetings. Conflicts based on different facts and different views of facts are extremely valuable. Conflicts based on experience and data can be researched, validated, verified, reinterpreted, and discussed until common ground is identified. Team collaboration and consensus skills apply here.

Members Like to Test Ideas.   This is the gadfly phenomenon, and many teams have at least one. Although he or she may be annoying, the gadfly is another important and valuable source of conflict. Challenges, contrarian views, nay-saying, and off-the-wall hypothetical examples offer an opportunity to thoroughly examine the consequences of a decision. People who ask penetrating questions that seem to go against the grain of the consensus are serving a purpose, and they should be brought into the process. Team collaboration and consensus skills also apply here.

Some Members Have Different Values and Beliefs.   Like the gadfly, members with different values and beliefs force the team to look hard at their decisions. For example, a decision involving flexible work hours would not be valid unless a working parent with child-care responsibilities brought work and family issues to the team table. Or a team deciding on promotion criteria may not have considered all aspects of the decision until they have incorporated the views of a disabled employee. Different views, even nonconformist views, are vital to teams. If such views are not presented at the team meetings, they should be actively sought.

Five Ways to Resolve Conflict

Try these different methods when a healthy conflict of ideas and opinion challenges the team. The methods are:

1. Bargaining.
2. Problem Solving.
3. Voting.
4. Research.
5. Third-party mediation.

Let's take a closer look at each of these five methods:

1. Bargaining.   This is a method most people are familiar with. Bargaining is simply a matter of "If you do this, I'll do that." Call it horse-trading, basic politicking, dealing, or negotiating. Bargaining usually resolves conflicts through compromise.

How to Do It

- Before you start bargaining, identify what your bargaining chips are, that is, what you're willing to give up.
- See if you can do the same thing for the other side. Speculate on what their bargaining chips are.
- At the same time, decide your absolute minimum acceptable resolution, the limit of bargain beyond which you simply cannot go.
- Start the process by presenting the least valuable of your bargaining chips. Offer it ("If you do this, I'll do that"), and see what happens.

Think through these questions: What types of conflict in your team can be effectively handled by bargaining? Why would bargaining help conflict resolution in your team? Why would it hinder conflict resolution?

_____

_____

_____

2. Problem Solving.   This is one of the most objective ways of dealing with conflict. The key is to get different sides to define the real problem everyone is trying to solve. Once the problem is clear, the team can apply team collaboration skills to develop alternatives. Also, identifying the problem may highlight misunderstanding within the group.

How to Do It

- Make sure everyone involved in the conflict participates in the problem-solving process.
- Restate the goal of the team in trying to resolve the conflict. "Remember, our purpose is to raise money for the fund drive as quickly as possible."
- Ask each side of the conflict to present its view. Probe for facts that have led to those points of view and avoid arguing.
- As a result of hearing these different views, state the problem. "We have two different opinions about how to ask employees for money. One is direct and demanding, requiring a specific amount, the other is more open ended. Is that our problem?"
- Develop alternatives, using team collaboration skills. Be creative and encourage all members to participate.
- Evaluate the alternatives and select one that works for everyone.

Think through these questions: Problem solving is probably one of the most effective methods for teams to use in resolving conflict. Can you identify a current conflict or anticipate a future conflict that can benefit from a problem-solving approach? Why does identifying the problem clearly sometimes immediately provide a resolution to the conflict?

_____

_____

_____

3. Voting.   Yes, simply voting for one side or the other is a legitimate way to resolve conflict. It's the parliamentary approach. Of course, there are winners and losers in a voting situation, so there are some distinct disadvantages. A voted resolution to a conflict may have even less support than a compromise. Special care should be given to selecting which conflicts are appropriate for resolution through voting.

How to Do It

- Ask the team whether it thinks the conflict should be voted on. Discuss the consequences.

- State the problem as a yes-or-no question. For example, "Should we increase overtime for each member of the team?"
- Ask for a vote, count the yeas and nays. Your team may decide a two-thirds majority is necessary or simply a majority.
- If necessary, ask how winners and losers feel.

Think through these questions: Has your team ever voted on a conflict? What were the consequences? How would you recommend the team do it differently, if it had the chance? If you haven't voted on a conflict, what would be a likely conflict to vote on? What are the risks and advantages of voting?

_____

_____

_____

4. Research.   Many teams argue about issues on the basis of lots of opinion and few hard facts. One objective way to resolve these endless discussions is to gather data through research and interpret the findings. If the findings are inconclusive, then either conduct more research or accept the ambiguity and start problem solving.

How to Do It

- Before conducting research, define the fundamental question that needs to be answered to resolve the conflict. This is called the research question.
- Select an appropriate method. There are many different types of research:
    Conduct focus groups: ask other teams or groups what they think.
    Review documented records: examine and analyze historical data.
    Interview different people: ask questions, gather other opinions.
    Experiment: Collect data on an existing process, analyze it, and draw conclusions.
    Conduct a survey or questionnaire: Reach a larger group through paper-based methods.

Think through these questions: Under what circumstances should your team conduct research to resolve a conflict? What resources do you need inside and outside your team to help you do the research? Would the results be available in time to affect the team? What happens if members disagree on the interpretation of the findings?

_____

_____

_____

5. Third-Party Mediation.   When conflicts within the team reach a point of inflexibility, the time may be right to seek the counsel of an objective third party. Objectivity is key. If the mediator appears biased, either toward one team member or a particular point of view, the process is undermined. For this reason, the team should be particularly wary of going to the boss to break a deadlock.

How to Do It

- The team should identify who the objective, third-party mediator should be.
- Before the mediation process, all parties must agree to abide by the results.
- During mediation, each side will present its facts and opinions. The mediator will ask questions.
- A good mediator will try to facilitate problem solving among the conflicting parties. Only when this fails to reach a breakthrough will the mediator make a final determination.
- The team should reflect on the process, seeking to learn how to avoid the inflexibility that led to mediation instead of a team-generated resolution.

Think through these questions: What are some of the benefits of mediation? What are the risks? Who would be a good mediator for any conflicts within your team? How can you tell when it's time to seek a third party? Why is mediation a last resort?

_____

_____

_____

Trust Makes Conflict Work

When team members trust each other, the inevitable and expected conflict among team members becomes an opportunity to foster new thinking and creative ideas. Without trust, conflict can disable a team's progress toward its goals.

Why is trust so critical? The level of trust among team members affects how ideas are generated, how decisions are made, how conflicts are resolved.

Think for a moment of a situation in which a team member or other person *lost* your trust. What happened to your working relationship?

_____

_____

_____

As you have learned from experience, when trust between people is lost, it affects how they work together, and it is extremely difficult to regain. In the absence of trust, members withhold information, guard their comments, exclude people from discussions, and resist conflict resolution.

To effectively manage conflict, as well as do all the other things teams do, all members must act in a way that fosters trust.

5

How do you build trust? Think of someone you really trust. What is it about them that lead you to trust them?

_____

_____

_____

Team members build trust by how they act both in team meetings and in other settings. Check off the trust builders that are important to you. Remember, these actions work together to build trust:

- ☐ Consistently meet commitments: Do what you promise to do. Walk the talk.

- ☐ Bring reliable information to the team: You can build trust when what you are talking about is accurate and based on experience and data.

- ☐ Demonstrate skill at whatever it is you do. Team members tend to trust people who are competent.

- ☐ Show a sincere interest in the views, talents, and involvement of other team members. One of the qualities of a team is the blending of unique talents. People trust team members who show an interest in them.

- ☐ Make balanced judgments that attempt to account for the differences among the team. As the team matures and grows used to working together, individuals seem to drop extreme viewpoints and think almost as a group.

☐   Support the team and its decisions to others. Team members earn the trust of others when they defend, explain, and otherwise endorse the work of the team when it is challenged by others. To do otherwise—by bad-mouthing or second-guessing—undermines the team.

It is easy to lose the trust of your team: Would you trust someone who met some, but not all, of his or her commitments? What about a team member who, frankly, didn't know what he or she was talking about? When someone is supportive in a team meeting and then criticizes the team to a nonmember, what happens to trust? What would it be like trying to resolve a conflict about even as trivial a matter as when the team takes coffee breaks, for instance, with someone who practiced these trust-eroding activities. Lack of trust makes conflict resolution extremely difficult.

TRUST SELF-ASSESSMENT

To what extent do team members trust you? You can get a rough view of how others trust you by completing this self-assessment from the point of view of another team member. Pick someone with whom you may have had a conflict. See how their perception of you may get in the way of having a healthy discussion about conflicting views. This team member (you):

	Always	Sometimes	Never
Consistently meets commitments?	☐	☐	☐
Brings reliable information?	☐	☐	☐
Demonstrates skill?	☐	☐	☐
Shows a sincere interest in others?	☐	☐	☐
Makes balanced judgments?	☐	☐	☐
Supports the team?	☐	☐	☐

Were you frank and honest in your self-assessment? Are any ratings sometimes or never in the eyes of your team? If so, identify how you can earn an always rating on those that need improvement.

List three actions you can take to boost your rating:

_____

_____

_____

■ Expanding What You Have Learned

Think through these questions:

1. Can you have a conflict in a team without emotion? Why? Why not? Can you have cooperation without conflict?

_____

_____

_____

2. Research is an important technique for resolving conflict. What recent team conflicts have you experienced that would have benefited from historical research? How does looking back on past experience help resolve current conflicts?

_____

_____

_____

3. Do members of your team share the same goals and rewards? If not, what kinds of conflicts stem from this discrepancy? If they do, what effect do mutual goals and rewards have on the team?

_____

_____

_____

4. Review the things team members can do to build trust. What else contributes to building trust in your team? What kind of people does your team admire and presumably trust?

_____

_____

_____

5. How can a team help members become more flexible in conflict situations? What consensus techniques can be applied?

_____

_____

_____

Chapter Checkpoints

Conflict and Cooperation

✓ Conflict is natural—view it as an opportunity.

✓ Manage conflict toward productive discussion, not arguments.

✓ Avoid unnecessary conflict by using your team constitution.

✓ Clarify rules and procedures.

✓ Resolve conflict by:
   Bargaining.
   Problem solving.
   Voting.
   Research.
   Third-party mediation.

✓ Develop trust. This is the secret ingredient that makes conflict productive.

✓ Conflict can lead to greater cooperation.

6 | A Typical Team Meeting

This chapter will help you to:

- Apply some team skills to a case situation.
- Learn tips for making typical meetings more effective.
- Offer advice to a team as it works through different agenda items.

Two Workers, Two Meeting Experiences

Two production-line workers meet in the break room. Marty is from the painting section and Harry is from manufacturing.

Marty

We just had another team meeting this morning.

Harry

So did we.

Marty

Well, don't sound so enthusiastic.

Harry

Why should I? It was another dull, boring hour.

Marty

Really. What are your meetings like?

Harry

Are you kidding? The team leader reads all the memos we're supposed to know about, asks for questions and then we go back to work. It's an hour's worth of trying to stay awake.

Marty

That's too bad. Our meetings are much more lively. In fact, they're intense.

Harry

Are we working for the same company? What goes on in your meetings?

Marty

Everything. I don't think an hour a week is going to cover it any more. We've got to review last week's work, talk about what's happening, how to avoid errors, things like that. We never have enough time.

Harry

Hmm. Maybe I am missing something. ∎

Two employees, two different meeting experiences. For many members of work-unit teams, the weekly team meeting is the only chance they have to connect with the work and obtain a larger perspective of the business. Instead of being a one-way communication from boss to employees, more and more team meetings are settings where members can discuss issues and decide on new action plans. In fact, team meetings are the launching pad for the team skills you've been reading about.

In this chapter, you'll explore the kinds of activities that happen in team meetings and you'll have a chance to sit in on a typical team meeting to offer your advice and suggestions just like an actual member, using your new team player skills.

WHAT HAPPENS IN TEAM MEETINGS?

Team-meeting agendas are as varied as the kinds of things teams do. Let's break what generally happens into five categories: announcements, progress reports, problem solving, decision making, and planning.

Announcements.   Parts of team meetings are dedicated to announcing information for administrative purposes. That's what makes up most of Harry's meetings. Someone in the organization is using the team meeting to "pass the word." These are typically messages like: "Parking will be prohibited in the loading area while the garage doors are being repaired"; "Please change item number 23445 to 3421-B"; or "The western sales region has sold 10,000 units of our new product to General Acme, Inc." How do you think announcements can be made maximally effective?

_____

_____

_____

It's probably a good idea to reproduce the announcement in memo form and hand it out at the meeting. Members can state what they have to do as a result of the announcement and write those actions in their calendars or schedules. Another idea is to for a team member to volunteer to follow up a message if it's important enough. Sometimes these announcements don't matter much to the team, so the team can make good use of an announcements corner on the team bulletin board.

Progress Reports.   Another agenda item is often reporting progress on a project. A member gives a progress report stating accomplishments, obstacles overcome, results, and the like. Sometimes, the team is asked to think about how to get around a persistent problem, offering ideas to the member responsible for the project. Can you think of what team members ought to avoid in making a progress report?

_____

_____

_____

Progress reports can get bogged down in digressions and distractions. The danger is turning the progress report into a project meeting. Members who spell out every single detail can soon consume too much valuable meeting time. "So, we met last Wednesday evening, the night it was raining so hard. Let's see, Helen, Mark, Denise, and Bruce were in attendance. Our agenda was. . . ." Get the picture? Also, if not carefully monitored, discussions can go astray. "You need volume data on vendors? We did that about three years ago. I can get you the reports from Karla. She's really super. She's been working down in Parts for the last year and a half. You know, she must have spent a month pulling that data together. That was before we had computers down there. Ever try to do that by hand? Well. . . ." Progress reports should be crisp and clear, using a format something like this:

- Review project purpose.
- State current status.
- Identify issues and problems.
- Ask for assistance, if needed.
- State next milestone.

Problem Solving.   One of the most frequent agenda items in a team meeting is problem solving. For example, one of the team members presents performance data for the previous week. Something is not right—there are too many errors or defective parts being produced. The team spends its time analyzing causes of the problem and developing solutions.

This is a perfect setting for applying team collaboration skills—asking lots of questions to explore and define the problem, getting ideas out on the table, developing creative solutions. Everyone participates, innovative ideas spark discussions, and what-if scenarios test different approaches. Problem solving can be great fun, but what can throw a damper on the experience? Can you identify what can happen in a team meeting to stop problem solving cold?

_____

_____

_____

The person who listens to creative ideas with a very sour expression, as if saying, "This guy is nuts," or "Why would we want to do that?" can put an end to any creative problem solving, at least for that meeting. So does the member who says, "Yes, but. . . ." or, "We did that already" or, "Come, on, let's get serious." When ideas are criticized as they are being expressed, team members will soon learn to avoid criticism by stopping the flow of original suggestions.

On the other hand, problem solving in teams that are truly good at it can be enormously rewarding and productive. The key is to open up the discussion to ideas and let them flow: quantity counts.

In problem solving, much team discussion revolves around testing different ideas, pointing out the consequences of acting on one alternative versus another, and improving ideas until the problem winds up being solved.

Decision Making.   Another major agenda item is decision making. Inevitably, the team will be faced with a number of choices. The members have to choose from among alternative courses of action. For example, "Should we ask our boss's boss to our next meeting?" "Should we tell every customer to complete the customer satisfaction survey form when they check out?" "Should we put the new manual in a three-hole binder or should we just staple it?" These represent typical decisions that a team has to make—decisions that will benefit from conscientious application of team consensus skills.

What do you think is the biggest decision-making pitfall for a team? Can you identify what can happen in a team meeting to stop decision making cold?

_____
_____
_____

Making decisions based on opinion not grounded in experience or facts can be a difficult chore, indeed. Opinions are all right when they are based on experience, maturity, or hard-won wisdom. On the other hand, when members bring facts to the table, decision making can be less of a guess and more of a calculated risk. It's worth noting that no team decision is absolutely right. In fact, the decisions teams make tend to be more right and less wrong.

Planning.   Every team meeting involves some kind of planning. Planning results in the To-Do list that is developed throughout the meeting. When a team plans its next steps in a team meeting, assignments are made, deadlines are set, resources are identified, and support is enlisted. "Who'll reserve the room for our customer demonstration session?" "Is there anything else we have to do to implement these pricing changes?"

In a way, planning is like problem solving. The problem is implementing the decisions and ideas generated in the meeting. Brainstorming plays an important role in planning. Not surprisingly, teams can get very creative not only about what they plan to do but also about the how—steps to take to put the idea to work. Do you know what makes plans work?

_____
_____
_____

Effective planning includes at least five elements:

- Actions to take, in sequential order if appropriate.
- Support and help needed, including people and other resources.
- Anticipated obstacles and ways of overcoming them.
- A progress review date.
- Indicators of success or ways of telling that the plan is working.

You may have other ideas about what to include in an effective plan. The idea is to anticipate all the possible different outcomes and account for them in your plan.

TEAM MEETING ROLE PLAY—PULL UP A CHAIR

We've seen that team meetings include announcements, progress reports, problem solving, decision making, and planning. Now, let's sit in on a typical team meeting. See if you can play the role of a team member. Read the events, and as you come to a question, think about what you'd do or say.

Background. This team is a group of clerical workers in the claims department of an insurance company. Each worker has several different duties, such as entering data from handwritten claim forms into a computer system, assigning a price or payment amount for each claim, and writing letters to customers asking for more information so the claim can be processed.

Welcome to our team meeting! Take a seat.

Each week, the team meets for an hour at 8:30 A.M. Tuesday morning, to review how many claims the group processed in the previous week and how many letters were sent out. Generally, team members analyze the different performance measures, suggest improvements, and resolve obstacles as they arise. This is a self-managed team. The manager of the unit sits in as a team member. Other members take turns facilitating the meeting.

Make believe you're a visitor, sitting in from your current job. Although new to teams, you understand the ideas behind constitution, collaboration, consensus, and cooperation. Got the picture? Come on, let's not be late.

The Weekly Team Meeting

Location: Conference Room B

Time and Date: Tuesday Morning, 8:30

Attendees: Six claims processors, one supervisor

8:30. Most members are present and ready at start time. As usual, the agenda is written on a whiteboard. Some special topics for discussion are starred. This week's team leader reviews the agenda, introduces you, the guest, asks if anyone has additional agenda items. No one has. What's this? Someone has just come in after the meeting has started. The team leader looks at you and asks, *"Have you got any ideas about how we can get started on time?"*

Response 1. You say, "To make sure meetings start on time, I would:

_____

_____

_____

_____

8:33. The manager reports last week's performance data—the number of claims processed, the number of letters sent, the number of complaints and compliments received. Each important parameter is compared to established standards developed earlier in the year. As the data are reported, they are plotted on graphs. Everyone knows the important parameters by heart and looks forward to each week's report. The manager looks at you and asks, *"Why do you think its important for us to post our weekly results on graphs?"*

Response 2.   You say, "I think it's important to post weekly results on graphs because:

_____

_____

_____

_____

8:37.   The graph shows the number of pricing errors last week was too high, well above the acceptable standard. This means clerks are paying either too much or too little for different kinds of claims. The team discusses what might have caused the increased error rate. One member points out that a change in pricing policy late last week was not communicated to clerks in time. "When it was communicated, it was mentioned verbally. We never got a memo. I guess the errors come from not implementing the new policy properly." Someone looks at you and asks, *"Have you got any ideas that might help us explore this problem?"*

Response 3.   You say, "I don't know the details of how things work here, but I do have some general questions that might help explore the problem of why new policies are not being implemented properly. The first one is:

_____

_____

The second one is:

_____

_____

8:40.   The group agrees that the problem came from poor communication of policy change. Several members offer different ideas for improving the communication of pricing-policy changes to clerks. You notice some members aren't contributing. *How would you encourage them to contribute?*

Response 4.   You say, "I would encourage team members who are not contributing by:

_____

_____

_____

8:45.   The team seems to agree that verbal communications have to be backed up by handouts outlining the new procedures and the clerks should keep a log of the changes in their manuals. There are also some unusual ideas about writing changes directly on-line so that clerks can have access to the latest news every morning. Another idea is to install a large whiteboard in the work area to note the most recent changes. The team leader says, "There are four ideas on the table: handouts, keeping a personal log, on-line access, and the whiteboard. *How do you suggest we come to agreement on the ideas that are best?*

Response 5.   You say: "To reach agreement, I suggest the first thing you should do is to:

_____

_____

_____

8:48.   The team is deadlocked. Keeping a personal log of pricing changes is the idea that has emerged as the quickest and easiest to implement. However, some team members are having trouble with the idea of a personal log. "Does that mean if I make an error and I have no record of the change in my log, it's okay?" asks one member. "What if I was sick and I didn't record the change, and I process work with errors?" asks another. "I don't want to get penalized for something I didn't know about." Apparently, to some team members, there is more to this than meets the eye. The team leader looks to you, asking, "The personal log makes sense but there is resistance. *How can we gain consensus for this simple idea?*"

Response 6.   You say, "I would gain consensus by:

_____

_____

_____

8:52.   The team agrees with the idea of the personal log with certain changes to ensure fairness for everyone. The next agenda item is determining when each member can attend a customer service training program. Because of the need to keep up the processing rate, the sessions are scheduled at the beginning and end of the day. "There are two openings in the evening session, which goes until 5:30 or so, and four openings for a breakfast-hour session. Who wants to go when?" The question soon creates a conflict. In the discussion, members talk about child-care, after-school classes, transportation problems. The team leader asks, *"Have you got any ideas for solving this conflict?"*

Response 7.   You say, "I think a technique you might use to resolve this conflict is:

_____

_____

_____

9:10. With a reasonable schedule for the customer service training program worked out after a vigorous discussion, team members seem anxious to end the meeting. The final agenda item is to hear a report from one member on an ongoing project: The Action on Complaints Committee. The team sends a representative to this cross-functional committee each week to review customer complaints and develop policies. This week, the representative says the AC committee wants all teams to develop and test a new form for recording complaints. The team discusses what should be on the form. The project soon breaks down into drafting a prototype with the help of the graphics department, reproducing the form for the team, collecting filled-out forms and analyzing the data. The team leader asks, "Who wants to do what?" Several members volunteer for different tasks. The supervisor leans over to you and whispers, *"How can we make sure this project will be done right?"*

Response 8. You say, "One way to make sure members follow through on their assignments is to:

_____

_____

_____

9:25. The team is starting to squirm. There are still two items on the agenda. One deals with a report from management citing the impact of making personal phone calls at times when inbound call volume from customers is heavy. The other item is the introduction of a new instruction booklet that customers will use to fill out their claim forms. It has been designed using input from groups like the team you're meeting with now and is intended to reduce avoidable errors by customers. The team leader looks at you and says, *"We're out of time and there are two items left on the agenda. Any suggestions?"*

Response 9. You say, "If you're out of time, I would:

_____

_____

_____

9:30. The meeting is over and members are leaving, smiling at you as they go. One young man comes up and says, "I'm going to be the team leader for the next meeting. Based on what you've seen here, *can you give me any advice for improving how we work together?"*

Response 10.   You say, "Sure, here're two tips to improve the meeting next time:

_____

_____

_____

RESPONSE REVIEW

The last exercise was a way for you to get practice as a participant in a simulated meeting. Was this a demanding exercise for you? Participating in discussions right from the start is critical to your success as a team player and to the team's success in meeting its goals. Fortunately, in teams that work effectively, participation gets easier and more fun as you get used to it. Your advantage is that you are aware of how the team player skills can make the whole team more effective.

Here are some possible answers to the exercise. Compare them with yours, but remember that there's no one right answer.

Response 1.   "To ensure team meetings start on time, I would establish and enforce a ground rule in the team constitution that says meetings will start on time. How that rule is enforced depends on the enforcement your team can agree with. One idea is to simply close the door at the beginning of the meeting. Anyone who is late is not admitted. Some teams fine members who are tardy a small amount of money. Let your team decide."

Why is showing up on time so important? Actually, it's a small way of demonstrating commitment to the team goal and showing that members take the work of the team seriously. In addition to having to buy a lot of coffee as a penalty, members who are chronically late send a message about what they feel about the team's work. Can questions about trust be far behind?

Response 2.   "I think it is important to post weekly results on graphs because everyone in the work unit should know how the team is doing in achieving its common goals. Posting results reinforces those common goals and their importance. The technique of posting important results is called _visible management_. Team members can see where the team stands and can observe the trends emerging over time."

Response 3.   "I don't know the details of how things work here, but I do have some general questions that might help explore the problem of why new policies are not being implemented properly. The first one is. . . . The second one is. . . ."

In general, questions that begin with *Who, What, When, Where, Why,* or *How* are effective in exploring problems. Here are some effective questions that can start the collaboration process: *How often are changes made? Who decides what changes to make? What do other groups do when changes occur? Where do clerks currently note changes? When do errors occur?* These questions and their answers allow members to see the problem more clearly. Once the problem is clearly defined, the team can more easily begin to collaborate on a solution.

Response 4.   "I would encourage team members who are not contributing by directly asking for their opinions. While team members may initially be shy or cynical about the team's authority to get things done, the team process cannot work without their input and involvement. Stimulate participation with such phrases as, "What do you think, George?" "What do you like about that idea?" or "Let's go around the room to collect ideas.""

Response 5.   "To reach agreement, I suggest the first thing you should do is examine each alternative, decide what people think are the advantages of each approach, as well as the drawbacks. The point is, each member should contribute to the discussion. As the alternatives are discussed, a clear choice may emerge. If not, advantages and disadvantages that were not apparent at the beginning of the meeting will surface."

Response 6.   "I would gain consensus by asking all team members to describe what the personal log means to them and what they see as implications in its use. Once these differences are in the open, a discussion will clear up any misunderstandings and highlight potential flaws in the idea."

For example, since being absent on a day when pricing changes are made can lead to further errors, the team decided to back up the personal log system with a memo board, where all notices of changes recorded. Members returning from an absence are asked to check there first before working on any claims. The group agreed to that idea.

Response 7.   "Here is a technique you might use to resolve this conflict. First, gather as many facts as possible. Use the research technique before the meeting to collect, catalog, and analyze all members' obligations before and after work and perhaps their level of flexibility. Trying to schedule meetings without this information makes for a very confusing discussion. With a potentially volatile topic, such a lack of information may lead to unnecessary conflict. Once the data are clear, the team can engage in problem solving and even bargaining to arrange schedules."

Response 8.   "One way to make sure members follow through on their assignments is to build a ground rule into the team constitution that states members accepting projects and assignments will only take the work if they can complete the task. Members who say they will do something and who either don't do it or do it inadequately are letting the team down. Members should understand the team depends on them to be team players outside the meeting setting as well as in it. Other ways to guarantee follow-through include holding quick and frequent update meetings, asking people to work in groups of two or three—members will supervise each other—and pointing out the consequences to the team of not following through."

Response 9.   "If you're out of time, I would use any one of these ideas: ask the team to decide to stay for five more minutes, carry over unfinished items to the next meeting, deliver the messages via memo, examine the task required—for example, reviewing the new customer instruction booklet— and ask the team if they would do it as an individual assignment."

Meetings that frequently run too long could indicate other problems. The team may be trying to accomplish too much, or discussions may be wandering and unproductive. Announcements and other administrative messages better covered by memo may be taking too much discussion time, or the time allotted for meetings may be too short. One common time-consumer in team meetings is over-explaining administrative messages—sometimes reading them verbatim—when a headline phrase and a handout will more than do the job.

Response 10.   "Sure, here are two tips to improve the meeting next time. The team spent at least half the meeting solving the pricing-error problem, using performance data from the previous week. That was certainly a major priority of the work team, and it was time well spent. But the time spent scheduling when individuals should attent a training session could have been reduced by researching personal schedules and requirements beforehand.

Also, when people are waiting for a meeting to end, after solving work-process problems and discussing schedules, introducing anything new is anticlimactic. The administrative memo about personal phone calls and the new instruction booklet for customers seemed like add-ons in the last few minutes of the meeting. When planning agendas, first get the easy administrative announcements out of the way quickly, with as little discussion as possible. Then address the major issues."

Remember, the two constraints you have are the time your team has and the attention span of individuals.

Expanding What You Have Learned

Now, ask yourself these questions:

1. How would you feel if you were a team member of the meeting you just attended?

_____
_____
_____

2. What things did you see in this team meeting that you would like to use in your own meetings?

_____
_____
_____

3. Of the different activities that can take place in a team meeting—announcements, progress reports, problem solving, decision making, and planning—what does your team do most frequently? Is that all right? What activities should be practiced more frequently? Why?

_____
_____
_____

4. What other activities besides the ones mentioned take place in your work unit? What is the purpose of those activities?

_____
_____
_____

5. If you mentioned training or skill improvement as an additional activity, are enough time and attention paid to individual proficiency, or does the training take on the characteristics of an announcement? How can training be effectively conducted in the work unit?

_____

_____

_____

6

Chapter Checkpoints

The Meeting Process

Effective team players use their skills to make sure meetings are conducted smoothly. Keep in mind that most meeting are made up of combinations of:

✓ Announcements.

✓ Progress Reports.

✓ Decision-making sessions.

✓ Planning sessions.

Don't spend too much time on the announcements portion of a meeting. Listening to one person read a memo can be a waste of time.

✓ Keep progress reports focused.

✓ Involve everyone in the problem-solving process.

✓ Ground decision making in facts.

✓ Ensure that plans are realistic and feasible.

7 | Dealing with Team Problems

This chapter will help you to:

- Identify the most common problems teams face.
- Prescribe solutions that a team member can implement.
- Anticipate what problems your team may encounter and develop ideas for preventing them.

Just as a doctor diagnoses an illness from the symptoms, a team member should be able to identify the real problems being faced by a team. The team skills—constitution, collaboration, consensus, and cooperation—all represent "prescriptions" you can use to untangle the emotions, confusion, and conflict that may stop teams from being effective.

In the following exercise, you'll be given various problems and the indicators you may see in the work setting. Your job is to identify the problems and determine how you would handle them if you were a member of the team. This is an opportunity to practice applying the team skills.

Ready to begin? Read the situation and the indicators, then identify what you think the problem is and prescribe a solution. In your solution, first note what general team skills apply (constitution, collaboration, consensus, or cooperation) and then outline your specific suggestions.

Problem	What You See	Possible Causes	Potential Solutions
1. Lack of dis-agreement in team meetings.	Ideas accepted with minimal discussion. Reluctance to challenge ideas. Few questions on consequences.		Team skill(s): Suggestions:

7

Problem	What You See	Possible Causes	Potential Solutions
2. Commitment to the team tapers off after four or five meetings.	Members skip meetings or send "representatives." Lack of support or open undermining of team decisions. Members appear withdrawn or preoccupied at meetings.		Team skill(s): Suggestions:
3. Open conflict, blaming, and arguing divide the group.	Emotional discussions. Hurt feelings. Trust problems begin to erode relationships.		Team skill(s): Suggestions:
4. Ideas are flat, unoriginal, and typical.	Members seem satisfied with minimal efforts at creativity. Low volume of ideas is generated. Little time is spent thinking; there are few jokes, and not much laughter is heard.		Team skill(s): Suggestions:
5. Rambling, undisciplined discussions.	Points are repeated several times. People talk a lot without making new points. Discussions digress from the topic.		Team skill(s): Suggestions:
6. Individuals remain inflexible and defensive about their points of view.	Discussions reach an impasse. Emotions start to build. "Camps" and cliques divide the team.		Team skill(s): Suggestions:
7. Members don't/won't implement what the team decides to do.	Work goes on unchanged. Members "forget" team decisions. Members criticize the team to others in hallway chatter.		Team skill(s): Suggestions:
8. Team expectations are not in line with reality.	Team decisions are unrealistic and unworkable. Members want to change too much too quickly.		Team skill(s): Suggestions:

Problem	What You See	Possible Causes	Potential Solutions
9. Important stakeholders are not involved with the team.	Information for making decisions is missing or hard to find. Decisions are shot down before they can be implemented.		Team skill(s): Suggestions:

CHECK YOUR RESPONSES

Here are some sample responses to the situations you've been working on. See if you agree with these potential solutions to team problems.

Problem	What You See	Possible Causes	Potential Solutions
1. Lack of disagreement in team meetings.	Ideas accepted with minimal discussion. Reluctance to challenge ideas. Few questions on consequences.	The team may not be comfortable with positive conflict, so members avoid disagreement. Also, the team may not have expected risk taking and frank speaking as a part of team work.	Team skill(s): Constitution, cooperation. Suggestions: Members should agree to disagree. The team constitution should state that members are expected to speak frankly without penalty. Give members training in conflict resolution.
2. Commitment to the team tapers off after four or five meetings.	Members skip meetings or send "representatives." Lack of support or open undermining of team decisions. Members appear withdrawn or preoccupied at meetings.	The honeymoon is over, and the hard work is starting. Many teams experience growing problems after buckling down. Two major causes: (1) the benefits of achieving the team goal haven't been sold, (2) operating ground rules are not working.	Team skill(s): Constitution, collaboration. Suggestions: Members should hold an organizational meeting to review ground rules and the team goal. Confront members with their team responsibilities. Solve schedule-conflict problems. Ask members to state their commitment to the team.

Problem	What You See	Possible Causes	Potential Solutions
3. Open conflict, blaming, and arguing divide the group.	Emotional discussions. Hurt feelings. Trust problems begin to erode relationships.	Blaming and negative conflict are violations of the team constitution. Also, members may feel they are not being heard.	Team skill(s): Cooperation, constitution. Suggestions: The team needs to review conflict-resolution techniques as well as the team constitution rules about disagreeing without being disagreeable.
4. Ideas are flat, unoriginal, and typical.	Members seem satisfied with minimal efforts at creativity. Low volume of ideas is generated. Little time is spent thinking; there are few jokes, and not much laughter is heard.	Members may not be aware that innovation and creativity are allowed and that open expression of diverse ideas is needed to address problems. Also, corporate culture frowns on fun at work.	Team skill(s): Collaboration. Suggestions: Anyone can be creative if given permission. The team needs to review collaboration skills, even conduct a few silly exercises, like naming new uses for a marshmallow. Get away from the work setting.
5. Rambling, undisciplined discussions.	Points are repeated several times. People talk a lot without making new points. Discussions digress from the topic.	The team leader may not be controlling the discussion. Members feel they can't tell others to stick to the subject. The purpose or outcome of the discussion was not made clear when it began.	Team skill(s): Consensus, Constitution. Suggestions: Some new ground rules for this team may be to limit discussion, make a priority of defining the decision needed and how it will be reached. The team leader can also review meeting-facilitation skills.
6. Individuals remain inflexible and defensive about their points of view.	Discussions reach an impasse. Emotions start to build. "Camps" and cliques divide the team.	When members dig their heels in, look to how the discussion process is working. Are members talking openly about the issues? Are facts and opinions based on experience the basis for discussion, or are members reacting	Team skill(s): Consensus, cooperation. Suggestions: It's time to call a break, remind the team about their shared goal, and use team consensus skills to clarify differences and identify similarities.

Problem	What You See	Possible Causes	Potential Solutions
		from emotion? Do members understand where the others are coming from?	Time spent discussing differences reduces resistance and opens the possibility for creative solutions. Perhaps an outside facilitator should conduct some meetings.
7. Members don't/won't implement what the team decides to do.	Work goes on unchanged. Members "forget" team decisions. Members criticize the team to others in hallway chatter.	Team decisions may not be clear or specific. Also, members may not be enrolled in the goals of the team or realize the importance of those goals. Clearly, personal commitment is an issue.	Team skill(s): Cooperation. Suggestions: Divided loyalties and conflicting priorities can make life hard for a team member. If the ground rules for participation are clear, the team should confront wayward members with the need to commit. Doing so can lead to creatively resolving priority conflicts.
8. Team expectations are not in line with reality.	Team decisions are unrealistic and unworkable. Members want to change too much too quickly. Team makes decisions the manager should have made.	This team may not have clear direction, boundaries, and guidelines.	Team skill(s): Constitution. Suggestions: This team should review its goal and, with the manager, clearly define roles and responsibilities. Several test cases can be examined.
9. Important stakeholders are not involved with the team.	Information for making decisions is missing or hard to find. Decisions are shot down before they can be implemented.	Even work-unit teams may not see the need to include representative members from other departments.	Team skill(s): Constitution, collaboration. Suggestions: Conduct a stakeholder analysis. Review everyone involved with the decisions the team makes. Include them as members of the team, either full-time, part-time or on a one-time basis.

7

■ Expanding What You Have Learned

Now, apply your diagnostic abilities to your own team. Think about the answers to the following questions:

1. In which of the team skills—constitutions, collaboration, consensus, cooperation—do you feel most competent? Least competent? What can you do to improve your competence level?

_____

_____

_____

2. Which of the team skills do you feel most confident about applying in a team setting? Least confident? How can you build your confidence?

_____

_____

_____

3. Which of the team skills do you think will be most valuable to your team, either now or in the future? Are any team skills not valuable either now or in the future?

_____

_____

_____

4. How can you use team skills to avoid problems you can foresee for your team?

_____

_____

_____

Chapter Checkpoints

Hooray for Team Players!

✓ Use your team skills for all types of problems.

✓ Everyone can be a team player—don't exclude anyone from the process.

✓ Practice, practice, practice effective application of team skills.

✓ Collaborate with your teammates to resolve common, shared problems.

✓ Teamwork increases everyone's effectiveness.

✓ Effective team players:
    Push an organization to soar beyond its goals.
    Keep customers satisfied.
    Are fulfilled employees.

8 Relax—You'll Love Your New Identity

This chapter will help you to:

- Assess how comfortable you are with the team taking over or participating in traditional management tasks.
- Identify the management tasks your team can begin to take on immediately and those that need to wait for the team to develop additional skills and capabilities.
- Develop a task-focused plan to develop team skills and gradually involve the team in more management activities.

Ode to Bosses with Teams and Sympathy:
(From Chief to Coach Potato)

Once you were a boss, with a clipboard, a cubicle, or a door.
Not too long ago, people waited for you to tell them the score.
You were responsible, all-knowing, accountable.
If you said, "Make these changes," that request was insurmountable.
If you said, "Bill, work with Sally this afternoon,"
Bill worked with Sally, and none too soon.
The director, an expert, you were the chief.
Your command and control were beyond belief.
You knew, they knew, who you were.
And, Oh, how the office did purr.
Now you're a facilitator, but your team doesn't invite you to talk.
It was hard, it was traumatic when they told you to take a walk.
You have to influence, advise, and empower.
You have to support and have visions by the hour.
And you need soothing, reassurance you'll not fail.
"Will the numbers be met? Will the quality prevail?
Will someone find out I'm not useful at all?"
You're just a coach potato waiting for a team to call.

If you're a manager in an organization where teams, participatory management, and empowerment are finding a place in your work unit, you
may be having an identity crisis. Oh, things may not be as bad as they are
for the manager in the poem, but you may be questioning your role.
Changing how decisions are made, how work improvements are implemented, and all the other things you used to do by yourself does create a
sense of discomfort. After all, aren't you responsible and accountable for
the performance of the work team?

So far, this book has focused on how to be an effective team player. All
of the team skills apply to you because, after all, you are a team player both
in a cross-functional management team and in your own work-unit team.
This chapter is devoted to the manager's changing role in the culture shift
to a team-oriented environment. This chapter shows you a systematic way
of looking at your role in relation to team activities, and it will give you
some guidelines for being the manager of an empowered work team.

First, let's find out what your comfort level is with involving teams in traditional management activities.

COMFORT-LEVEL RATING SCALE

Establishing direction and priorities
My comfort level for involving team members is:

Very High	High	Moderate	Low	Very Low

Deciding *what* to do in the work unit
My comfort level for involving team members is:

Very High	High	Moderate	Low	Very Low

Deciding *how* to do it
My comfort level for involving team members is:

Very High	High	Moderate	Low	Very Low

Planning next steps
My comfort level for involving team members is:

Very High	High	Moderate	Low	Very Low

Monitoring/Checking Progress
My comfort level for involving team members is:

Very High	High	Moderate	Low	Very Low

Deciding on corrective action
My comfort level for involving team members is:

Very High	High	Moderate	Low	Very Low

Providing rewards and recognition
My comfort level for involving team members is:

Very High	High	Moderate	Low	Very Low

8

In the space below, list the areas where you are most and least comfortable in involving the team.

Most Comfortable	Least Comfortable

HOW TO BE MORE COMFORTABLE

As a manager or supervisor of a team-oriented work unit, you are still accountable for results. The best advice for managers who face the challenge of developing empowered teams is first to recognize where you feel comfortable and where you have discomfort, and then to develop a way to help the team evolve. Here's a three-step approach.

1. Identify opportunities for involving the team where you feel comfortable.
2. Develop individual team player skills to take on tasks.
3. Gradually add responsibilities as the team's capabilities grow.

No, managers do not have to turn over the keys of the business to the team. The process of developing the team should be evolutionary, not revolutionary. Now, does that make you feel more comfortable? No? Let's take a closer look at how to develop the team.

Look at the table at the top of page 93. Down the left side are the management tasks traditionally done by you, the manager. Across the top are examples of how different groups typically reassign these management tasks. At the intersections, a "T" indicates what the team does and has responsibility for. An "M" shows what the manager does. Self-directed work teams, for example, do most of the tasks associated with running their work unit, although establishing direction and priorities are most likely a management task. In contrast, manager-led teams have fewer traditional management tasks. You decide what your team should get involved in and when. See, you really do have some control here.

Take a moment to identify what kinds of management tasks your team can become involved in doing right now. Mark them with an "R" for "right now." Then, indicate the tasks the team can do with some development and those which the team is not likely to be doing in the future, either because of your personal comfort level or the culture of the organization. Mark those tasks with a "D" for "development" or an "N" for "not now."

You're on your way to creating a task-based plan for phasing over different management roles to the team. This plan, by the way, is under your control. Now that should make you feel a little better.

Representative Task	Self-Directed Team	Employee-Involved Team	Manager/Supervisor Led Team	Your Team
Establish direction and priorities	M or T	M	M	
Decide what to do in the work unit	T	T	M	
Decide how to do it	T	T	T	
Plan next steps	T	M and T	M and T	
Monitor/check progress	T	T	M	
Provide rewards and recognition	T	M	M	

After you've completed the table, work out your plan. In developing team members, think of the team skills—constitution, collaboration, consensus, cooperation—that you feel are most appropriate to the management task. In completing the planning form:

- List those management tasks you can ask the team to do now.
- Identify those management tasks that the team can become involved in with some skill development and coaching.
- Specify the team skills to help that development.
- Estimate the date when the team can expect to give the task a trial.
- List those skills that you want to reserve for yourself or your supervisors, at least for now.

MANAGER'S PLAN FOR IMPLEMENTING TEAM PARTICIPATION

Tasks Team Can Do Right Now	Tasks to Develop	Team Skill(s) to Focus On*	Date of Implementation Trial	Tasks Reserved for Later Consideration

(continued)

MANAGER'S PLAN FOR IMPLEMENTING TEAM PARTICIPATION

Tasks Team Can Do Right Now	Tasks to Develop	Team Skill(s) to Focus On*	Date of Implementation Trial	Tasks Reserved for Later Consideration

* Team skills: constitution, collaboration, consensus, and cooperation.

Guidelines for Managers of Empowered Work Teams

Here's some advice gathered from managers like yourself, who are dealing with the shift to an empowered team environment.

First, focus on your priorities as a Team Manager.

1. Get clear on the organization's vision and direction; decide how to translate this direction into priorities and goals for your work unit.

2. Establish performance standards for the work that reflect internal or external customer requirements. After initial standards are created, the team can use them as a benchmark to start its process-improvement efforts.

3. Develop the team's capabilities, specifying what the team is empowered to do today and the skills it needs to develop in order to add other tasks in the future.

4. Ensure that individual team members have the work skills to do their jobs today, and prepare them for new job skills required tomorrow.

Second, become an excellent team facilitator and coach.

1. Steer team meetings, don't drive them. The key here is asking for input as you go along. For instance, instead of giving orders ("We're going to move the furniture"), give members a chance to

provide input ("We're going to move the furniture. Any ideas on how we can do that quickly and without disrupting the work flow?")

2. Let the team talk without saying, "Yes, but." Don't edit what people say in team meetings, don't cut them off. Allow discussion to happen.

3. On the other hand, learn how to control discussions. Don't allow rambling and repetition. Move the team through the issues to a definite conclusion. When making decisions, make sure the team knows what the criteria are to consider in making a choice, that is, expense, resources, time, and so forth.

4. Frequently remind the team who the customer is. Refocusing on the customer is often a way of making priorities clear for the team.

5. Don't make decisions that the team should make for itself. Learn to push appropriate decisions down. Breaking dependency on the manager is an important step in creating empowered teams.

6. Finally, be a cheerleader. Learn to say, "Yeah!" and "Sure, let's try it and see what happens," and "Yes."

Finally, learn to be an effective team player yourself.

1. Team members will expect you to practice what you preach. Learn the team skills presented in this book as well as others not addressed. As a manager, you are already a team member of different management and cross-functional teams. If you play your cards right, your team might let you be a part-time member, instead of just a leader.

2. Define your own role as team player. Hint: Managers make great resource-gatherers and messengers to higher levels.

3. Try to adjust. Teams are really good for you and the organization.

BENEFITS TO THE MANAGER

What are the benefits to you, the manager, when you make the changes needed to shift to an empowered team environment? Managers remain responsible and accountable for results, but in a team environment, the team shares that responsibility. A major benefit to involving teams and empowering employees is that you don't have to do it all by yourself.

Teams create a surprising sense of energy and enthusiasm in the workplace. If you nurture this energy and keep it focused on the work, members will be happier and results will startle even you. In fact, productivity and quality will go up. Don't be surprised if cost and waste go down. Research shows that's what happens when teams share responsibility for getting things done.

Finally, the quality of work life will be better. Guiding, developing, and leading people is more rewarding in the long run than dispensing orders. Although you still have responsibilities and accountabilities, your stress level will probably go down, your evenings and weekends will be family time again, and you'll feel closer to your team members and colleagues.

Expanding What You Have Learned

Use the answers to the following questions to help you reflect on your role as manager in an empowered team setting.

1. What rewards do you get from being a manager in a hierarchical setting? In other words, what do you like about being the boss? Is it telling people what to do? Think about it.

_____
_____
_____

2. If you were asked to actually do the same tasks your employees do every day, what improvements do you think you'd suggest in the work process? Do you think your employees see the same opportunities? Have you asked them?

_____
_____
_____

3. Who is your customer, internal or external? Do your team members know who their customer is? What would the customer say about the quality of work done by the team?

_____
_____
_____

4. What resources can you bring to team meetings? What can you do outside the team setting to support the team decisions? What would it take for you to support the team's decisions at higher levels of management?

_____

_____

_____

5. How do you feel about supporting team decisions that you are not fully bought into? What would it take to gain your full commitment? Under what circumstances should you let team members know you have reservations about their decisions?

_____

_____

_____

8

Chapter Checkpoints

Managers and Empowerment

For many managers, making the transition to a team environment can be distressing. But making the switch to empowered teams can be seen as a process controlled by the manager, not a process with a life of its own. Remember that a shift in the managers' role doesn't mean that managers are no longer important:

✓ Goals still need to be met.

✓ People and teams still need direction.

✓ Resources and development are still crucial.

Managers can learn to turn over some activities to the team and retain other responsibilities. The benefits of a well-functioning team far exceed any liabilities. Many managers believe that teams:

✓ Get the best work done.

✓ Ensure quality products and services.

✓ Keep customers *and* employees happy.

Post-Test

Assess your understanding of how to be an effective team player by answering the following questions:

1. The three characteristics of a team are shared purpose, people having to work together, and _____.

2. After defining its goals, a new team should spend time writing the team _____.

3. Laughter is an indicator that the team skills of _____ are being used effectively to solve a problem.

4. When a team is reaching a decision, a _____ is a preferred outcome rather than a compromise.

5. If team members can manage it, _____ can actually contribute to better decisions.

6. If team members don't arrive at meetings on time, the team should examine the team _____.

7. Announcements, progress reports, problem solving, decision making, and planning are common team meeting _____.

8. Team members have achieved a _____ when individuals feel committed to a decision.

9. Anyone involved with a problem can become involved in the team _____ process that results in a creative solution.

10. A _____ is anyone who is affected by the decisions of a team and should have a say in deciding the final outcome.

ANSWER KEY

1. Pay-offs or benefits for everyone.
2. Constitution.
3. Collaboration.
4. Consensus.
5. Conflict.
6. Constitution.
7. Activities.
8. Consensus.
9. Collaboration.
10. Stakeholder.

The Business Skills Express Series

This growing series of books addresses a broad range of key business skills and topics to meet the needs of employees, human resource departments, and training consultants.

To obtain information about these and other Business Skills Express books, please call Irwin Professional Publishing toll free at: 1-800-634-3966.